# COMPLETE BOOK OF ETHNIC JOKES

SANFORD TRIVERTON

A HART BOOK

GALAHAD BOOKS • NEW YORK

PUBLISHED BY
A & W PUBLISHERS, INC.
95 MADISON AVENUE
NEW YORK, NEW YORK 10016

LIBRARY OF CONGRESS CATALOG NO. 81-80072
ISBN: 0-88365 - 542 -X
MANUFACTURED IN THE UNITED STATES OF AMERICA

# COMPLETE BOOK OF ETHNIC JOKES

# CONTENTS

# PREFACE

Ethnic jokes are as old as the hills.

An ethnic joke attempts to downgrade the people of a culture dissimilar to your own. The English are portrayed as slow-witted, the Irish as pugnacious, the Scottish as stingy, the Italians as sloppy, the Germans as rigid, the Poles as stupid, the Jews as money-grubbing, the Blacks as lazy, the Americans as crass, and the Frenchmen as sexy.

Today, nobody of sound mind subscribes to any of these aspersions. Everybody knows that there are slow-witted Frenchmen, dumb Americans, rigid Italians, sexy British, etc.

Yet in every nation on earth, the ethnic joke continues to thrive. The Northerner calls the Texan boastful; the Southerner pictures the Yankee as sharp; the Midwesterner finds the Okie stupid; and everyone denigrates the folks who live in any area other than his own.

Ethnic jokes are told by the amateur vaudevillians of our day. These jokes impart a pleasant feeling of superiority to the listener.

No one, of course, takes these jokes seriously. Certainly, the compiler of this volume doesn't. These jokes are not meant to offend—merely to amuse.

In recent years, there has been a spate of stories about Poles. So endearing is this humor that sometimes even people of Polish descent tell these stories. The plain fact is that today no one really believes the stereotype, and despite the onslaught of Polish jokes, the regard for

Poles has never been higher than it is today during their struggle for freedom.

The stories in this collection have been chosen because we think they are funny. Change the names—from Finkelstein to O'Sullivan, from Stanislavski to Williamson—the jokes are *still* funny.

The use of dialect has been avoided because dialect makes for difficult reading. The storyteller may supply as much actual dialect as he is capable of.

SANFORD TRIVERTON

# COMPLETE BOOK OF ETHNIC JOKES

# American Jokes

Two young soldiers had tied one on in a local bar and had lost their way back to their Orlando base. Suddenly one of them bumped into an object in the dark and was knocked off his feet. "Hey, I think we've gotten into a cemetery," he remarked. "Here's a gravestone."

"Whose is it?" asked his buddy.

The soldier lit a match, peered at the stone, and said, "I don't recognize his name, but he sure lived to an old age—225."

"Wow!" his friend exclaimed. "Who was it?"

The first soldier lit another match. "Some guy named Miles to Miami."

## Would You Believe It?

This story concerns a particularly persistent suitor. He lived in Chicago and courted a girl in Oshkosh for two years.

Things somehow went wrong and she wouldn't see him any longer. So he took to the mails and he sent her a special delivery letter three times a day for 33 days.

On the 34th day, his strategy produced results. The girl eloped with the mailman.

## Place Utility

It was after the second World War had ended. Joe Dink was still in Japan waiting to be discharged. His wife, Irma Dink, was wild with anxiety and jealousy because she had read about the goings on between the American soldiers and the Japanese girls. Finally she could stand it no longer, and she wrote her husband. "Joe, hurry up and come back. What do those girls have anyway that the American girls don't?"

"Not a thing," wrote back Joe, "but what they have got, they've got here."

## Cure

A man came to a doctor complaining that he had an uncontrollable cough. The doctor gave him a bottle of castor oil and said, "Go home and drink down the entire bottle, and come back tomorrow."

When the patient came back the next day, the doctor asked, "Did you take the castor oil?"

The man answered "Yes."

The doctor then continued, "Do you still cough?"

The patient said, "Yes, I continue to cough."

The doctor gave him a second bottle of

castor oil and said, "Take this, and come back tomorrow."

The next day, the man returned. The doctor asked him, "Do you still cough?"

And the patient said, "Yes, I still cough regularly."

The doctor then gave him yet another bottle of castor oil and said, "Drink this entire bottle tonight and come back tomorrow morning."

The patient returned, and the doctor looked at the poor wretch and said, "Do you cough now?"

The patient quiveringly answered, "I don't cough anymore—I'm afraid to."

The Texan visiting Vermont asked a farmer how large his farm was.

"Oh, it's rather large," the Yankee replied, "about 200 yards in that direction and nearly 300 in that."

The Texan chuckled. "Back home in Texas," he said, "Ah have a house at one end of my ranch. Ah can get into my car at the house, step on the gas, and at the end of the day Ah still won't have reached the other end of the ranch."

The Yankee farmer nodded sympathetically. "Yeah, I once had a car like that, too."

## Smart Cookie

Two morons met on a city street.

"I'll bet you you can't guess what I've got in my hand," the first said.

"A zebra?" asked the second.

The first glanced in his closed hand for a moment, then said, "No, try again."

"A jeep?" the second guessed.

"No," replied the first. "Try again!"

"A bear!" cried the second.

"Right," said the first. "What color?"

"Pink," the second answered.

"Ah!" said the first, "You peeked!"

Bud and Jerry, two truckdrivers from the Midwest, drove to Pennsylvania for a week of deer hunting. When they arrived at the main hunting lodge in the area, however, they learned that there were no vacancies. But since they'd traveled so far, they decided to stay and go hunting anyway.

That evening, they knocked at an isolated farmhouse and asked the woman who answered the door if she would be willing to rent them rooms for a week. Although she was a widow and all alone, she agreed.

About eight months later, Bud called Jerry at his home. "Jerry, I just received a wire from a lawyer in Pennsylvania, and frankly I'm puzzled. Just tell me one thing. By any chance did you have an affair with that farm widow?"

"Well, Bud, I meant to tell you about that."

"And did you happen to give my name to her?"

"Well, er, I meant to explain that, too."

"Well, don't bother. The widow died and willed her farm to me."

**A** group of Peace Corps volunteers were being briefed before leaving for a remote African country.

"Now, boys," the instructor told them, "you may very well run across some poisonous snakes where you're going, and one of you could be bitten. Let me say, first of all, that no matter what you've heard, drinking whiskey is no antidote. If you're bitten by a snake, you must make a cut near the bite so that it bleeds freely. Then put your mouth over the gash, and suck out as much blood as you can."

"But, sir," one recruit called out, "suppose you're bitten on the backside?"

The instructor stared back and cracked a grin. "Then, my boy, you'll find out who your friends are."

## Answer That!

In the midst of a furious downpour, a young lady pulled up at a motel to spend the night. "I'm sorry," the hotel clerk told her, "but we don't have another empty room. I just rented the last room, a double, to that young man over there."

The lady, realizing that this was the only motel within miles, approached the young man: "The clerk told me that you just rented the last room," she said. "I have nowhere to stay tonight and it's raining too hard to drive. You don't know anybody that I know, and I don't know anybody that you know, so would you mind if I occupied one of the beds in your room?"

The young man agreed.

That night, when they had climbed into separate beds and turned out the light, the lady said, "It's kind of cold near the window here, and your bed is wide enough for two. You don't know anybody that I know, and I don't know anybody that you know, so would you mind if I moved over into your bed with you?"

The young man said he had no objection.

A few minutes later, the young lady spoke again. "You don't know anybody that I know, and I don't know anybody that you know, so how about having a party?"

The young man shrugged. "If you don't know anybody that I know, and I don't know anybody that you know," he said, "then who can we invite?"

## Now You're Talking

Danny was an inveterate bargain hunter. He hadn't a penny to his name, but whenever he saw a bargain he couldn't resist it.

One day a friend of his came to see him. Jim said, "Danny, I've got a terrific bargain for you. A boatload has arrived for the Barnum and Bailey Circus and they have an overstock. They've got an elephant on board, a baby elephant, that's worth at least $2,000 and I can land it for you for only $300."

Danny looked at Jim as if he were half crazy. "What! An elephant! An elephant in my one-room apartment? You must be out of your mind! In the first place, there's no room for it. And in the second place, how could I feed it? In the third place, what could I do with it? Don't be nuts!"

"But," persisted Jim, "I'm telling you this elephant is worth 2,000 bucks and I can get it for you for a mere 300, maybe even for 250."

Danny was adamant. "Get the hell out of here, will you? You're off your rocker. I don't need an elephant. I don't want an elephant. Leave me alone with elephants."

But Jim knew his friend and he continued hammering away. "Listen, Danny," he said, "the fact is they have an overstock. You know, I think if I put it to 'em I could get you two elephants for the same 200 bucks."

"Now you're talking!" said Danny.

**M**oore spotted Miller at the clubhouse bar one afternoon and rushed over excitedly. "I've heard about the tragedy you experienced last weekend. It must've been terrible!"

Miller sipped his martini and nodded, lowering his head with the unpleasant memory. "I was playing a twosome with old Mr. Crawford," he murmured solemnly, "and the poor guy dropped dead on the seventh green."

"And I heard you carried him all the way back to the clubhouse," Moore said, admiration gleaming in his eyes. "That was quite a job. Old Crawford must've weighed at least 250 pounds."

"Oh," Miller replied, sipping again, "carrying him wasn't difficult. What tired me was putting him down at every stroke, and then picking him up again."

## A Few Minor Errors

Two farmers were chatting in front of the bank. "I hear you made $60,000 in alfalfa," said the first.

Not wishing to be impolite, his friend replied, "Well, that isn't quite right. It wasn't me, it was my brother; it wasn't alfalfa, but oats; not $60,000 but $6,000; and he didn't make it, he lost it."

An imaginative executive of a New York credit service sent the following letter to one of his delinquent accounts:

"Dear Sir:

After checking our files, we note that we have done more for you than your mother did—we've carried you for 15 months!"

## Honesty Pays

"I've been unfaithful to my wife," Lenny told his friend, "and my conscience can take no more. I'm going to confess to my wife tonight and beg her forgiveness."

That night Lenny told his wife about his extra-marital flings. Naturally she was hurt.

"Was it Mrs. Wilson?" she asked. "I know she cheats on her husband."

"I won't tell you," Lenny replied.

"Was it Mrs. Harris?"

"No, I won't say."

"Was it Mrs. Williamson?"

"Sorry, but I can't tell you."

"Well," retorted the angered wife, "if you won't tell me who they are, I won't forgive you."

The next day Lenny ran into his friend, who asked if his wife had forgiven him.

"No, she didn't," Lenny explained, "but she gave me three swell leads."

## Lucky Break!

To increase circulation, a certain newspaper advertised an accident policy free to all new subscribers. A few days later, this advertisement appeared in the paper:

"P.J. Melton subscribed to our paper and was given a free accident policy. On his way home from work, he fell down a flight of stairs and broke an arm, a jaw, and both legs. The accident policy paid him $1,000. *You may be the lucky one tomorrow.*"

**A** Kentucky mountaineer wrote to a mail-order house to ask the price of toilet paper. He received a letter directing him to look on page 241 of their catalogue.

"If I had your catalogue," the mountaineer wrote back, "would I need toilet paper?"

**"I** got insomnia real bad," complained a man to his doctor.

"Insomnia," said the doctor, "is insomnia. How bad can it be? What do you mean, 'real bad insomnia'?"

"Well," said the patient, "I got it real bad. I can't even sleep when it's time to get up!"

A backwoods inn boasted a modest sign on the porch: "Rooms to Let. Food. Country Atmosphere." The inn was hardly a sophisticated hotel, but one night a shiny black Cadillac pulled up in front of it. The owners of the car had gotten lost and wanted to spend the night there.

The man and his wife were big-city people in fancy clothes, and they emerged from the Cadillac as if they owned the world. Contemptuous of country life, but desperate for a night's lodging, the couple did not even pretend to like the idea of staying at the inn. They were above it all.

After registering at the desk, the couple entered the dining room of the inn. Ignoring the simple menu, the man plunked down a dollar and said, "For this, I want food, drink, and entertainment."

In a few minutes, the innkeeper returned with two slices of watermelon. "You asked for food, drink, and entertainment," he said. "Here it is. Eat the pulp, drink the juice, and play with the seeds."

Dorothy Parker and a friend were once discussing a celebrity whose garrulousness was unrivaled.

"She's so outspoken," observed the friend.

"By whom?" inquired Miss Parker.

Some people will go to great lengths to get out of something they'd rather not do. Others take a more straightforward approach.

An Iowa corn farmer once saw his neighbor coming up the road to visit. The neighbor wanted to borrow the farmer's brand new ax. The farmer hesitated. Then he said, "Sorry, Jim, I've got to use it to shave tonight."

The farmer's teenage son was mortified. He was close enough to hear the conversation, but he said nothing. Then at the dinner table he asked his father, "Dad, why did you give Jim such a silly excuse when he wanted to borrow the ax?"

His father replied, "If you don't want to do a thing, one excuse is as good as another."

## Magnanimous

The divorce court judge listened intently as the distraught wife charged her husband with non-support.

When she finished, the judge told the husband: "You obviously haven't taken proper care of this good woman, and I'm going to give her $25 a month."

The husband beamed with delight. "Why that's mighty nice of you, Your Honor," he said, "and I'll give her a dollar or two from time to time myself."

Deep in the Tennessee hills, a farmer's mule kicked his mother-in-law to death. An enormous crowd of men turned out for the funeral. The minister, examining the crowd outside the church, commented to a farmer friend, "This old lady must have been mighty popular. Just look at how many people left their work to come to her funeral."

"They're not here for the funeral," snickered the friend. "They're here to buy the mule."

Professor Michaels was conducting a class in physiology. He turned to one of his pupils and said, "Mr. Jones, will you kindly tell the class what organ of the human body exudes a liquid, expands to six times its normal size, and happens to be very tender."

Mr. Jones turned all colors and said, "Professor, I don't think it proper for you to ask me a question like that."

Professor Michaels turned to the class and said, "Ladies and gentlemen, this young man has evidently not done his homework. The proper answer to the question is the eye which exudes tears, and whose pupil expands to six times its normal size. It also happens to be a very tender organ. And as for you, Mr. Jones, you are suffering from delusions of grandeur."

Dorothy Parker always had the right words to quash the insufferably superior.

A comedian once entertained at a party to which Miss Parker had been invited. The man seated next to her, full of scorn, cast a withering look at the laughing guests.

"I'm afraid I can't join in the merriment," he drawled. "I can't bear fools."

"That's strange," Miss Parker chuckled. "Your mother could."

The *Steak au Poivre* was as tough as a leather apron. The irate diner called the waiter and snarled, "I want to see the manager!"

The manager came, and politely asked, "What's the matter, Sir? Is there anything wrong?"

"Yes!" fumed the customer. "This steak is terrible. It costs $14.50 and it's as hard as nails. You can give this steak to your chef and tell him to go shove it up his ass!"

The manager left—taking the steak with him.

In two minutes, he returned, and said, "I'm dreadfully sorry, sir. The chef says you'll have to wait. There's one *Lobster Thermidor* and one *Veal Cutlet Parmigian* ahead of you."

A lovely but rather flat-chested young woman visited a physician for her periodic physical examination.

"Please remove your blouse," the doctor told her.

"Oh, no," the young lady protested, "I just couldn't!"

"Come, come," the doctor replied, "let's not make mountains out of molehills."

## Just Make Sure

Warren's mother-in-law had passed away, and he called an undertaker friend to find out whether she should be embalmed, cremated or just buried.

Without hesitation, the friend replied, "All three. Take no chances."

It was in a hotel at Miami Beach. There was a sudden knock on the door. The lady jumped up out of bed and said to her lover, "Quick! It's my husband. Jump out the window!"

The lover gasped, "Jump out of the window? Why, we're thirteen stories up!"

The lady said, "This is a helluva time to get superstitious!"

## A Little Effort Needed

A feisty, overage delinquent once faced Judge Kenesaw Mountain Landis and tried to talk his way out of a five-year sentence for his misdeeds.

"But, Your Honor, I'll be dead long before that," complained the old man. "I'm a very sick man—I can't possibly do five years!"

"Well," the judge said firmly, "you can try, can't you?"

Two morons in a dark room were playing with a flashlight. One of them held it so that the beam of light hit the ceiling.

"I dare you to climb up that beam," he said.

But the other moron looked at him wisely and answered, "Ha, you can't get me to try a fool stunt like that. I know you—just when I get to the top, you'll turn it off."

The smallest Congressman ever to serve was Georgian Alexander Stevens. The Southerner was under five feet tall and weighed in at less than eighty pounds. But he wasn't short on wit!

One day, an angry opponent approached him, a six-foot-three-inch Congressman from

Texas whose bulk blocked Stevens' path. "You pipsqueak!" stormed the Texan. "Why, I could *swallow* you and never know I'd eaten anything!"

"In that case," replied Stevens smoothly, "you'd have more brains in your belly than you ever had in your head."

**O**ne of our more famous senior senators spent many years as a trial lawyer before running for public office. He says the most important thing he learned in the courtroom is the value of a brief speech.

He tells of the time he was opposed by a long-winded prosecutor who spent over four hours summing up the case for the jury on the hottest day in July.

When the time came for the future senator to sum up, he approached the judge quietly. The hum of the fans was the only sound in the courtroom other than that of the jurors taking out their handkerchiefs to mop their brows and stifle their yawns.

"Your Honor," said the lawyer, "I will follow the example of my friend who has just concluded, and will submit the case without argument."

He won the case.

## Lucky! Lucky! Lucky!

A lawyer had scheduled a business trip to New York, and a colleague had suggested he call on Miss Agatha Jane Foote while in town. "It'll be an unforgettable experience," the colleague promised. "She's no ordinary trollope, I assure you."

The first night of his New York stay, the lawyer took a cab and got out in front of one of the finest brownstones on Fifth Avenue. He rang the bell, and a maid ushered him in. After presenting his card, he was led into an elegantly furnished drawing room and invited to make himself comfortable. Miss Foote would be down shortly.

While waiting, the lawyer stepped over to a huge floor-to-ceiling bookcase and examined the gilt-bound works. Among the many tomes was a 40-volume set of *Corpus Jurus*.

A few moments later, Miss Foote stepped down the curved staircase in a most elegant evening gown. The lawyer stood stunned. She was indeed gorgeous!

But he was further stunned to find Miss Foote's conversation urbane, charming, and witty. He turned to the bookcase and remarked, "Miss Foote, I notice a set of *Corpus Jurus* on your shelves. Is it yours?"

"Yes," she replied, "I'm a graduate of the Columbia Law School."

"Is that so?" the lawyer continued, amazed. "Then, tell me, how did you ever get into this business?"

"Oh!" Miss Foote shrugged, "I must have been very lucky."

## Fair Enough!

A cop was crossing the Brooklyn Bridge. There was a man perched on one of the girders, ready to leap.

The policeman begged, "Please, mister, if you jump, I will have to jump in after you. It's freezing cold, and while we're waiting for the ambulance to come we'll both catch pneumonia and we'll both die. Please, mister, be a good fellow and go home and hang yourself."

One not-so-talented writer submitted a novel to a publisher based in New York. After a month went by without a reply, the writer sent a letter to New York. "Please report on my manuscript immediately, as I have other irons in the fire," he wrote.

The publisher wrote back, "We have considered your manuscript and advise you to put it with the other irons."

A factory in the Northwest operated on a single, huge electrical generator, and the plant fell into complete helplessness on the day the power source broke down. Repairmen tried everything possible, but without success. Finally, since inactivity was an extravagance the factory could not afford, the president sent to the parent company for an expert.

When the man arrived, everyone at the plant crowded around him. The president directed him to the generating room and said, "Jones, I hope you can help us." The man said nothing, but began to slowly examine every pipe, every dial, every switch on the generator.

Finally, Jones stopped in front of a particular pipe and produced a small hammer from his tool kit. His audience watched in awe. Gingerly, he felt with his fingers for the right spot. Then he tapped the hammer carefully at just the right angle. Immediately, the generator began to run again.

The president smiled in relief and said, "Well done, sir! And what is your fee?"

"Five hundred and five dollars," said Jones.

The president was suddenly prudent. "Five hundred and five dollars for simply hitting the pipe with a hammer?"

"Ah," explained Jones. "For that, five dollars. For knowing *where* to hit, five hundred dollars."

## Can You Blame Him?

Three old men were sitting together conversing. One thought a while and then said to the other two oldsters, "Who would you like to be buried with?"

The first said, "With Einstein, because he was one of the greatest geniuses the world has ever seen."

The second one said, "With John F. Kennedy, because he was one of the greatest Americans who ever lived."

The third one said, "With Diane Keaton."

"What!" said the other two. "You want to be buried with Diane Keaton? Why, she's not dead yet!"

"Neither am I," said the third gent.

## Unassailable Conclusion

A panhandler approached a gentleman and asked for a dime for a cup of coffee.

"Look at you!" the prospect snapped reprovingly. "You sleep on park benches, your clothes are a mess, and you don't even have ten cents for a cup of coffee. Why don't you get a grip on yourself and get a job?"

"Get a job!" the panhandler snarled in disgust. "What for—to support a bum like me?"

Senator Chauncey Depew was a likable man and had many admirers. His friends once arranged a dinner party for him, at which his praises were sung all evening long. Then Depew was asked to say a few words himself.

The senator was not one to mince words. He rose and said with a smile, "It's pleasant to hear these nice words while I'm still alive. I'd rather have the taffy than the epitaphy."

Ilka Chase had recently published her book, *Past Imperfect*, when she encountered a noted Hollywood actress at a party.

"I enjoyed your book," cooed the star saccharinely. "Who wrote it for you?"

"Darling, I'm so glad you liked it," Ilka replied shrewdly. "Who read it to you?"

A plebe at Annapolis sent a long letter home to mother describing his activities. Among other things he wrote, "One of the important things I have to learn around here is how to use my sextant."

The mother looked at the letter aghast, "My God!" she exclaimed, "Is *that* what they teach them in the Naval Academy!"

In many small villages, some public officials still perform several functions. One constable in a small midwestern town also operates as the local veterinarian.

Not too long ago, his wife took an anxious phone call. "Is Mr. Whittaker there?" a hysterical neighbor asked.

"Do you want my husband's services as a veterinarian or as a constable?" Mrs. Whittaker asked.

"Both!" exclaimed the neighbor. "We can't get our bulldog to open his mouth, and there's a burglar in it!"

A visitor from Boston got off at Grand Central Station in New York and jumped into a cab. It was 10 o'clock at night and the visitor hadn't eaten his supper. He was rather hungry.

The Bostonian was particularly fond of fish. He leaned toward the cabbie and said, "Tell me, mister, do you know where I can get scrod at this time of night?"

The cabbie scratched his head for a moment and answered, "You know, sir, in my 20 years in the taxi business, I've been asked that question over a thousand times; but I must tell you that this is the first time in all my experience that anybody has phrased that query in the pluperfect."

Former Chief Justice of the Supreme Court Charles Evans Hughes enjoyed the humor of one of the more modest Supreme Court Justices, Benjamin Cardozo. One occasion the Chief Justice recalled was a boat outing the Justices had planned in order to relieve some of their recent strains.

The dedicated Justice Cardozo, a man totally dispassionate in the courtroom, was losing an all-too-human battle with the steady rolling of the boat. Sympathetically, Chief Justice Hughes put his hand on his associate's back and said, "Can I do anything for you?"

"Yes," replied Cardozo, "overrule the motion."

## Easy Solution

Grandpa Jones, age 76, had announced his intention to get married, and his relatives were worried. Mae Belle, his bride-to-be, was only 21.

One of Grandpa's daughters finally laid it on the line. "Gramps, you know we're very concerned. Getting married at your age is definitely a hazard. It could be fatal."

"Well," Gramps chuckled, "I wouldn't fret over it. If she dies, I'll simply get married again."

Clarence Darrow's way with words was not restricted only to the courtroom.

A worried litigant found her troubles were over the minute she retained Darrow; the lawyer defended her brilliantly and won her case hands down.

When it was all over, the client said to him, "Oh, Mr. Darrow, how can I ever show my appreciation?"

"My dear woman," Darrow responded with equanimity, "Ever since the Phoenicians invented money, there has been only one answer to that question."

The lady on the plane was doing crossword puzzles, and seemed to be struggling over a few words. In desperation, she turned to the man sitting next to her and said, "Excuse me, but could you help me with this puzzle?"

"It's a four-letter word," the woman continued, "ending in the letters 'i-t.' The definition says that it's found in the bottom of a bird cage, and that the governor of this state is full of it."

The man replied immediately, "The word, Madam, is 'grit.'"

"Ah, yes, so it is!" the lady exclaimed. "Do you have an eraser?"

## Gotcha!

The golf pro came into the clubhouse, and was introduced to a new member. The new member said he'd like a game, but that he didn't shoot very well. The pro thought he would be an easy mark and said that his usual stakes for playing with anybody were $50 a match.

The new member replied that he hadn't any objection to the amount of the wager, but that since he was a very poor player he required a handicap.

"What handicap do you want?" said the pro. "I'll give you five holes."

"No," said the newcomer. "I don't want five holes, I just want two gotchas."

"Gotchas?" asked the pro. "What the hell are gotchas? I've heard of mulligans, and I've heard of all kinds of other handicaps, but I've never heard of gotchas."

"Well," said the newcomer, "if you want to play me for $50, that's what I want—two gotchas. I'll explain to you as we go on what gotchas are."

"O.K.," said the pro, believing that he could hardly lose to a dub like this one. The most he'd have to forfeit would be two holes.

So they proceeded to the links. The pro won the first four holes with ease. On the fifth hole—a par three—the newcomer hit his ball straight onto the green, and the ball trickled to within five inches of the pin. The pro also landed on the green, but his ball was seven feet away from the pin, a more or less routine putt for a club pro.

First, the pro lined up his ball carefully; then he examined the turf; then he bent over his ball with his putter. But just as he began to stroke the ball, the newcomer stole up behind him, and grabbed his testicles, and cried, "Gotcha."

Of course, the pro missed the putt. The dub won the hole, and the score was now 4 to 1.

About two hours later, both players came back to the clubhouse. The pro was asked by an old member how he made out with the newcomer. "I lost," he said, shamefacedly.

"You lost?" cried the other, incredulously. "How could you lose to that guy? He can't possibly get around the course in under 90!"

"Yes, I know," said the pro. "I should have taken him easily. But have you ever tried swinging at a golf ball while waiting for a second gotcha?"

**I**f all the freshmen at Yale were laid end to end—no one would be surprised.

Three men who had recently died were brought before St. Peter. "Tell me, how did you meet your death?" said St. Peter to the first.

The first man answered, "Well, I was executed for committing murder. I came home one afternoon, found my wife in a state of undress, looked around the house, found a smoldering half-smoked cigar, found a strange man's hat on the chair, accused my wife of infidelity, got a cockamamy answer from her, and then searched frantically around the apartment for her lover.

"I couldn't find him. Then, as I went to the window to cool off, I looked out, and right below the window I saw a man standing without a hat, smoking a cigar. The way he looked—so nervous, pacing up and down—made me sure he was the man. I looked around for something to throw at him. I wanted to kill him. I found nothing at hand. So in my rage, I lifted up the fridge, and threw it right out of the window. It killed him on the spot. I was adjudged guilty of murder, was executed, and so here I am."

St. Peter turned to the second and said, "Tell me, how did you happen to leave your earthly abode?"

"Well," replied the second man, "I really don't know for sure. Some six months ago, I was to meet a man on business on a certain street. I was late. When I got there, the man wasn't there. So I paced up and down nervously, looking in all directions, stamping impatiently. All of a sudden, I felt something was coming down on top of me. I looked up, and I saw a fridge within inches of my head. That's all I remember. Apparently, I was crushed to death on the street."

St. Peter then turned to the third man, and said, "Tell me, how did you get here?"

"Some months back, I had an affair with a married woman I had taken a fancy to. One afternoon, I visited her in her apartment. She told me her husband wouldn't get home until late that evening, but after we had made love, and I was sitting around smoking my cigar, he unexpectedly returned home. His wife cried out in a hoarse whisper, 'My god! Here comes my husband! Quick! Hide!'

"Where? I asked.

"In panic, she opened up her empty fridge, and I jumped in!"

## Propriety

He was an English teacher and she was one of his pupils. It was exceedingly dark when they parked in Lover's Lane.

After a little sparring, she exclaimed, "My! It's gruesome!"

"Such grammar!" he scolded.

## The Pretzel Hold

The scene was the last Olympic games. In the quarters of the American wrestling team stood John Mack, the trainer, warning his protégé, Mike "Bull" Flamm, about the forthcoming match.

"You know," Mack said, "the Soviet wrestler you're about to tackle, Ivan Katruvsky, is one of the greatest wrestlers in the world. But he really isn't as good as you are. The only thing he's got that makes him a terror is his *pretzel hold.* If he once gets a man in his pretzel hold, that man is doomed. He's used the pretzel hold on 27 competitors, and in each case, his opponent gave up within ten seconds.

"So, listen to me, Bull, you've got to be damned careful. Never let him get you in that pretzel hold. If he once clamps you in it, you're a goner!"

Bull listened carefully to Mack's instructions on how to avoid that crippling grip of Ivan's.

For the first three minutes of the bout, neither the American nor the Russian could gain an advantage. The crowd was on edge.

Then, suddenly, pandemonium broke loose. Bull Flamm had fallen into the clutches of Ivan's pretzel hold, and was moaning in agony. Mack, the American trainer, couldn't stand it. He knew the match was lost, and he left the arena in deep gloom. Down the corridor, the echoes of Bull's anguished cries still reached him.

And then, as Mack was about to enter his quarters, he heard an enormous shout arise from the stadium, a cheer the like of which he had never heard in all his long experience. The stands were in an absolute uproar. From the shouts, Mack knew that Bull had won the match. But he couldn't understand it. What could have caused the unthinkable turnabout?

A minute later, Flamm came trotting into the American dressing room. His trainer threw his arms around him, and said, "Bull, how in hell did you ever get out of that pretzel hold?"

"Well," answered Flamm, "he twisted me into such shapes that I never felt such agony in all my life. I thought my bones were going to break. And as I was just about to faint, I saw two balls hanging in front of me. With one desperate lunge, I bit those balls. Well, Mack, you can't imagine what a man is capable of when he bites his own balls."

## Biological Note

"Dear Sir," a man wrote to the editor of a country paper. "Can you tell me how long cows should be milked?"

His answer came back in the next mail.

"Just the same as short cows, of course."

A woman, who had been browsing around in a furniture store for an hour or so, finally decided to buy a certain bed, and asked the salesman, who had been following in her wake, to write up the order. But while he was writing it, she changed her mind, and decided to cancel the order.

Much embarrassed to tell the salesman who had spent so much time with her, she blurted out: "Sorry, I'm not going to take the bed. I think I'd rather have an occasional piece in the living room."

A lady of leisure stopped at a little town in the West. Her calling soon became known, and she received visits from the town's male population, young and old, married and single. So keen was the ardor of her admirers that they visited her again and again. In fact, she completely captivated the town.

Finally, the elders of the church met and determined to put a stop to the young woman's operations. The chief of police was on his vacation and the mayor would not act in the matter, so action devolved on the churchmen themselves. A committee of three headed by the deacon called on the girl.

"We must approach her gently," said the deacon, "and persuade her to leave without a scandal." When they got to her house, he again said, "Let us not alarm her by a show of force. You gentlemen wait down here, and I'll go up and speak to her."

But the moments turned into minutes, and the minutes turned into an hour, and still the deacon had not come down.

The two who waited for him began to grumble. After another half-hour, down came the deacon. "There is nothing for us to do here," he said, shaking his head, "this young woman has been grossly maligned. In the short talk I had with her, I found her to be a most cultured girl. We have no right to force her to leave town."

"All right," replied one of the others wearily, "button up your pants and let's go!"

## A Strict Constructionist

Arnold, nine years old, was walking up and down the halls of the school when he was met by the principal, who stopped him and demanded to know why the boy was indecently exposed.

"Well," answered Arnold, "in class this morning, I raised my hand, and said I wanted to go to the bathroom. My teacher told me to stick it out until lunchtime."

The intellectual young man was telling of his girl friend. "Jane," he remonstrated, "I don't think you're the girl for me. My interests are in art, in literature, and in music. You are only concerned with sports, with gambling, and with common activities that are altogether alien to me. In fact, to be blunt about it, you're downright uncouth!"

"Uncouth!" she exploded. "Me? *What are you talking about*? Uncouth? Didn't I go along with you to them operas, them concerts, them lectures, and all that sort of shit?"

George's wife was becoming suspicious as his hours became more and more irregular. One night his wife, determined to find out where he'd been spending his time, wired five of his friends: "George is not home. Is he spending the night with you?"

By the time George arrived home that night, his wife had received five telegrams all reading: "Yes."

Three priests went to Grand Central Station to get a train to Buffalo. The elder two appointed the youngest one to go to the counter to buy three tickets. Behind the wicket stood a gorgeously buxom young lady wearing a dress of outrageous decollete. The young priest was visibly flustered.

Finally, he blurted out, "Please let me have three pickets for Titsburgh."

When he realized what he had said, he was mortified, and ran back to the two other priests without buying the tickets.

The second took the money and approached the window. Here, he too encountered the same upset, but managed to say "Can I have three tickets for Pittsburgh?" And then, laying down a $50 bill, he continued, "And I'd like my change in nipples and dimes."

Realizing what he had said, he was so abashed he left the tickets on the counter, and ran back to the other two priests.

The third, the eldest, then strode up to the counter to ask for the tickets and the change. Scrutinizing at length the female clerk dressed in such a revealing fashion, he considered it his duty to admonish her.

"Young lady," he said, "you know if you go around dressed in such a provocative manner, you will most certainly obtain your just desserts in the life to come. It is my bounden duty to tell you that when you pass to the Great Beyond, St. Finger will certainly be there pointing his peter at you. . ."

## Lady, You Just Don't Understand!

A stately lady visited the zoo, and stared at the animals with great interest. Quite nonplussed, she pored over the signs in two adjacent cages and then asked the keeper, "Pray, sir, what is the difference between the American porcupine and the European porcupine? They look much the same to me!"

"Well," answered the attendant, "there's really no difference at all, except that the prick of the European porcupine is nine inches long, while that of the American porcupine is only seven."

Highly indignant, the lady trotted off in a huff to the curator's office. She demanded that the attendant be discharged.

"Oh!" the curator explained, "You misunderstood him. What he meant to convey was that the quill of the European porcupine is nine inches long, while the quill of the American porcupine is only seven inches long. As a matter of fact, neither one's prick is more than two inches long."

At a meeting of a congressional committee, one of the members made a motion for an appropriation of $768,000 for a bridge to be constructed across the Orentes River.

A senior member of the committee, a man

of seventy-five, objected and said, "Listen, Tom, that motion of yours is nothing more or less than outright pork barrel. There's no need to spend the taxpayers' money for some useless piece of steel to satisfy a few constituents in that backwoods county. As a matter of fact, the Orentes River—so-called—is no river at all; it's only a puny stream. Why, I could piss half way across it."

The congressman who had made the motion rose to his feet and heatedly declared, "The representative from Illinois is out of order."

The chairman turned to deliver his ruling when the older congressman jumped to his feet and yelled, "You bet I'm out of order! If I was *in* order, I could piss *all* the way across that little creek!"

**A** worried, middle-aged businessman went to visit his doctor. He wanted advice on how to live to be one-hundred.

"Well," said the doctor, "you'll have to give up smoking, drinking, and women."

"Will that make me live to be one-hundred?" inquired the businessman.

"No," said the doctor, "but it will make it seem like it."

**T**wo golfers were marking time before they could tee off. "I suppose you heard," said one, "that Timothy Brown killed his wife."

"Yes, I heard something about it," responded the other, "but how? How did it happen?"

"Oh, with a golf club."

"Oh, is that so? How many strokes?"

**A** salesman, told about a very fancy whorehouse on upper Fifth Avenue, arrived at the address and found a private mansion. He rang the bell and was met by a maid who, without saying a word, gave him a card. The card read: "Follow all instructions. Go into the waiting room, and proceed according to the signs."

The client entered a lavishly furnished salon, in which there were two doors. On one door, a sign read: "If you are over six feet, walk in here." The other one read: "If you are under six feet, walk in here."

Being less than six feet tall, the salesman entered the second door, and came into a smaller, but equally gorgeous, room. Here, too, he found two doors. On one door, there was a sign: "For men under fifty." On the other, there was a sign: "For men over fifty."

Being under fifty, he walked through that door, and came into another room which again contained two doors. On one there was a sign: "If your income is over $20,000 a year, walk through here." On the other door was a sign: "If your income is under $20,000 a year, walk through here."

Since his income was under $20,000 a year, he walked through the second door, and found himself on 86th Street.

## A Betting Man

Joe the gambler walked into a saloon and said to the bartender, "Bet you a dollar I can bite my right eye."

The bartender said, "O.K. It's a bet." So Joe took out his glass eye and bit it. The bartender paid up, and then challenged, "Bet you a dollar you can't bite your left eye."

Joe accepted the challenge. He then removed his dental plates from his mouth, and bit his left eye. The bartender smiled and paid up.

Then Joe said, "I'll bet you a dollar I can piss on you without getting you wet." This offer was promptly accepted, and then Joe proceeded to do his thing. The bartender jumped back, drenched, and exclaimed, "What the hell are you doing?"

"Well," answered Joe ruefully, as he slapped a buck on the bar, "You can't win em all!"

## Bad Connection

A guy with a quick temper got into a hassle with the phone operator because she couldn't seem to get him the right number. Finally, in utter exasperation, he yelled out, "You can take this phone and stick it up your ass."

The operator reported the incident to her superiors. Confronted with the company's complaint, the subscriber acknowledged that he had been somewhat unruly. But the company officials insisted that unless he apologized, they would promptly yank out his phone connection.

Being quite sore at the prospect of such an indignity, the subscriber refused to make the apology. The very next day, two men from the phone company came up to his apartment to pull out the instrument.

Now when the subscriber saw how things really stood, he was aghast. He just couldn't carry on business without a phone connection, so he decided to swallow his pride and apologize. He lifted up the receiver, got the operator whom he had insulted on the phone, and said, "Listen here, dearie. I'm terribly sorry. I know that yesterday I wasn't very nice. I told you to take my phone and stick it up your so-and-so. Well, dearie, you don't have to worry now. There are two men here to pull it out."

An analyst says to a patient: "You've been coming to me for two months because you say you have an inferiority complex, and I have been working as hard as I can to cure you of that notion.

"I am now ready to tell you that you *do not have* an inferiority complex. There's nothing for you to worry about. After talking to you day after day for two months, I am now completely convinced that you have no inferiority complex. The fact is, you're really inferior."

A hillbilly who came to register to vote was given a piece of wax paper and a ballpoint pen, and told to write his name on it. Of course, he couldn't do it.

The registration clerk said, "Well, you don't know how to write. Let's see if you can read." The clerk then handed him an Arabic newspaper and said, "Go ahead and read it."

"Well," the hillbilly answered, "I can't read the text. I can only read the headlines."

"Oh, you can?" sneered the clerk, "Go ahead."

The hillbilly then said. "This headline says that we hillbillies aren't going to vote this year."

## The Connoisseur

A sporting gentleman at a bar insisted that blindfolded he could taste any liquor and identify it, and tell the name of the company that produced it.

The bartender accepted the challenge. After the gentleman was blindfolded, the barflies gathered round to witness the first test. The expert took a sip, and immediately declared: "Four Roses, put out by Frankfort Distillers."

"Right," replied the bartender. They continued the test. On his next turn, the expert again took only one sip, and announced: "Canadian Club, put out by Hiram Walker."

"Right again," said the bartender. "Let's try just once more."

This time the gang thought they'd play a trick on him. Instead of whisky, the bartender filled the bottle with urine. When the expert tasted this, he remarked excitedly, "Why, this is piss!"

"Right you are!" acknowledged the bartender. "But whose?"

**A** young man was troubled by a passion which he had no prospect of relieving. He repaired to a pharmacist's to get a bromide. Somewhat embarrassed when he found a woman in attendance, he was about to leave when the lady behind the counter said, "Anything I can do for you?"

The young man was abashed but, after urging, finally blurted out that he had a perpetual hard-on. What could she give him for it?

"Wait a minute," said the woman, and went to the back of the store.

In a few minutes, the female pharmacist appeared. "I've just been talking it over with my sister, who is my partner," she said. "The best we can give you is the store and five hundred dollars."

**A** soldier on a crutch limped up to a soda fountain. The girl behind the fountain asked, "What'll you have?"

"A chocolate sundae," he said.

"Crushed nuts?" she asked.

"No!" he answered. "Just shot in the ass."

## So That's Where!

Two society ladies were chatting. "Whenever I'm down in the dumps," said Mrs. Worthington, "I get myself a new hat."

"Oh, yes?" responded Mrs. Catt, "I always wondered where you got them."

**A** man was reading the menu in a restaurant and asked the waitress, "What kind of soup do you have today?"

"Oh," she answered, "we have turtle soup and pea soup."

"I'll have turtle soup," he answered.

The waitress yelled into the kitchen, "One turtle soup."

But the diner said, "Just a minute. I changed my mind. Do you mind changing the order? Can you give me pea soup instead?"

"Of course," she said. And she yelled to the cook, "Hold the turtle and make it pea."

## You Can't Say She Wasn't Trying

Bottomley had gone broke. He had worked hard for 20 years, and finally his business folded.

His wife, Nancy, consoled him saying, "Bill, I'll never let you down. I'll get money for you. You'll start again in another business. I'll get you money. It's no shame to work for a living, and I'm going out on the streets."

Bottomley looked at her aghast. He thought she had gone out of her mind, but after she pleaded with him, and pointed out there was no other way, he agreed.

So Nancy left the house and didn't return for three days. She came home bedraggled, and placed 28 dollar bills and a quarter into Jim's hands. He looked at the money and said, "Who the hell gave you a quarter?"

"Why," his wife answered, "every single one of them."

One of the most unenviable positions in life is being last on a roster of after-dinner speakers. One elegant group of guests had already been subjected to a number of dull, drawn-out orations, when the host rose to introduce the last speaker.

"Wilton Lackaye, the famous actor, will now give us his address," he said.

Mr. Lackaye stood briefly. "Toastmaster and Gentlemen, my address is the Lambs Club, New York." And as he took his seat again, the audience applauded wildly.

"My poor husband," the woman sighed to her psychoanalyst, clutching her husband's hand. "He's convinced he's a parking meter."

The analyst regarded the silent, woebegone fellow and asked, "Why doesn't he say something for himself? Can't he talk?"

"How can he," the wife shrugged, "with all those coins in his mouth?"

A salesman fresh from a course in ballroom dancing arrived in Miami for a week's vacation. The first night he was in town, however, he received a wire from his home office that an emergency had arisen, and he would have to return on the morning plane.

He decided to make the best of his only night in Florida. Entering his hotel lobby that night, he spotted a gorgeous young woman seated in an armchair. He engaged her in conversation, and then invited her to go dancing.

The salesman danced impeccably, and the young lady was having difficulty keeping up with him. After about an hour, the salesman decided to be as blunt as possible.

"Look, Janie," he gasped as they danced madly, "I don't have much time. I have to be back in New York in the morning. Can't we speed things up between us?"

What do you expect from me!" she panted. "I'm dancing as fast as I can!"

Sam and Bill were seated in a subway. Sam turned around and saw that Bill's eyes were closed.

"Hey, Bill," he said, "What's the matter? I see you've got your eyes closed."

"Yes," answered Bill, "I just can't bear to see ladies standing."

One evening, Mrs. Scarlotti got into a cab. After riding a while, she suddenly realized she had forgotten to take along her purse, and didn't have enough money to pay the fare which now read $6.60.

"Driver," she cried out. "Stop! I don't have enough money to pay you."

"Oh, that's all right, called back the cabbie. "I'll turn down a dark street, and you'll take off your panties. . ."

"Oh, Mr. Cabman, you are going to get gypped," called back Mrs. Scarlotti, "My panties cost only 59 cents."

A girl came into a grocery and asked the storekeeper why cream was so much more expensive than milk.

"Well," answered the bright one, "it's because the cows find it so much harder to sit on small bottles."

Mrs. Hallaway was stunned to see her psychiatrist running down the street with a couch on his back.

"Doctor Stone!" she cried. "What are you doing?"

"Making house calls!" came back the reply.

The head of one Washington administration was approached by his secretary. "Sir," she said, "our files are becoming overcrowded."

"What do you suggest we do?" asked the busy administrator.

"I think we ought to destroy all correspondence more than six years old," answered the secretary.

"By all means," the prudent bureaucrat responded, "go right ahead. But be sure to make copies."

A taxi was creeping slowly through rush-hour traffic, and the passenger was already late. "Please," he told the driver, "can't you go any faster?"

"Sure I can," the hack replied. "But I'm not allowed to leave the cab."

Harry came East to visit cousin Ben in New York. Ben showed Harry the sights, and wound up the day by taking him for his first meal at the Automat.

Harry was delighted. He gazed at the display cubicles endlessly. His cousin, meanwhile, sat down to eat his meal. When he had finished and cousin Harry was still not in sight, Ben went to look for him. He found him at the apple pie slot, putting in nickel after nickel.

"Are you crazy?" exclaimed the cousin. "You already have fifteen pies!"

Harry chuckled gleefully and continued feeding coins into the machine. "So what does it bother you," he said, "if I keep winning?"

**C**hildren may be innocents, but they certainly pick up on everything they hear. One parent was listening to her six-year-old at her math lesson.

"Three plus one, the son of a bitch is four," he said. "Three plus two, the son of a bitch is five. Three plus three, the son of a bitch is six." The mother's jaw dropped in astonishment.

"Johnny, where in the world did you ever learn to talk like that?" she angrily asked.

"Oh, that's the way they teach us at school," said Johnny.

Unable to believe it, Johnny's mother visited the teacher and demanded an explanation. But the teacher was as horrified as the mother. She had no idea where Johnny had learned those words.

Then she realized what had happened. "I get it!" she laughed. "We teach the children to say, 'Three plus one, *the sum of which* is four. Three plus two, *the sum of which* is five!"

Sam Silverman had worked for most of his life in a Seventh Avenue sweatshop. During every February, when the days were wan and chilly, the members of Sam's union took a three-week vacation without pay, and went down to Miami.

They would come home with glowing stories. Sam dreamed of the day when he could afford to take such a marvelous trip to avoid the winter's cold.

In five years, Sam had saved up enough money to request an unpaid vacation. His request was granted. He flew down to Miami, registered in a small hotel, and stepped out into the full glare of Collins Avenue for a stroll. Then he sat down on one of the benches, to admire the beautiful palm trees. Within minutes, a woman sat down right beside him. She opened with a few questions, a conversation ensued, and the two soon became real chummy. Within an hour, they were in Sam's room, and they didn't emerge—neither of them—for three days.

Sam had the most wonderful time of his life. He came home ecstatic. Now he didn't mind his work, he was so full of memories of that marvelous vacation in Miami.

About four weeks later, a man called at the sweatshop and asked for Sam Silverman. The man was dressed in a dark gray suit, carried a briefcase, and had a business air about him. When Sam was pointed out, the man went straight to him, and said, "Are you Mr. Silverman?"

Sam said, "Yes, I'm Silverman."

"Well, then," said the man, looking him straight up and down, "I've got something I'd like to show you." He opened his briefcase, and spread on Sam's table six photographs which revealed Sam in the most compromising positions. Nude, Sam was rolling in bed with his lady-love, in that hotel room in Miami.

Sam looked at the pictures a moment, and then his face broke into a beautiful smile. "Mister," he said, "I'll take two of this, three of that, one of those, and four of this one!"

The young man was furious. He was taking his date to the ball game, and she had shown up an hour late. He'd still not spoken to her by the time they reached the ball park.

"How late are we?" she asked when they were seated, to break the ice.

"It's already the sixth inning!" her escort replied angrily.

"And what's the score?"

"Nothing to nothing."

"Oh, good," she cooed. "Then we haven't missed a thing."

The scene was a church dinner. A neighboring vicar had been called upon to deliver an address. Unfortunately, the man made too much of this invitation and spoke on and on and on. Everybody was bored to death.

Several notes had been passed to the speaker, advising him that his time was up, but he paid no heed.

Finally, the church treasurer picked up a napkin, scribbled a note, and confidently smiled as it was given to the speaker.

Immediately, the speaker stopped talking and sat down.

The chairman eagerly turned to the treasurer. "What in hell did you write?"

"Just four words," confided the treasurer. "'Your fly is open!'"

## You're Asking Too Much!

A successful young architect lived with his wife in a large Westchester ranch house, served dutifully by a Scandinavian cook, whom everyone praised as the best in town. One day, the cook, in tears, approached the lady of the house and told her, "I'm sorry, Madam, but I must leave on the first of the month."

"But why?" demanded the wife. "I thought you liked it here." The cook then bashfully explained that she had met a handsome soldier a few months before, and would soon be expecting a child. Eager to hold on to the talented cook, the wife immediately called her husband, then told the cook, "We've decided to adopt your baby."

A few months later, a daughter appeared upon the scene. The architect legally adopted her, and all was calm for another year, when the cook announced once again that she was leaving—this time due to an encounter with a young sailor. The architect and his wife discussed the matter, then told the cook, "It's not right to bring up a child alone. We'll adopt your second baby."

After the arrival of a darling little boy, all went smoothly for another two years, when the maid resigned again. The wife gasped, "Don't tell me that this time you met a marine."

"Oh, no, ma'am," replied the cook. "I'm resigning because I simply cannot cook for such a big family."

**A**t the turn of the century—before the era of yoga and jogging—one reporter asked New York Senator Chauncey Depew how he kept in shape.

Came the dour reply, "I get my exercise acting as a pallbearer to my friends who exercise."

It was a close and important baseball game.

Any disinterested spectator would instantly have decided that an umpire's life is not a happy one. But there were no disinterested spectators present. They were all rabid rooters and razzed the umpire unmercifully on every decision that went against the home team.

But the unruffled ump continued to call them as he saw them. In the ninth inning there was a close one against the home team that set the stands in an uproar.

One wrathful woman vaulted the grandstand rail and with blood in her eye charged on the ump. Restrained from physical assault on that unhappy official by two patrolmen, she shook her fist at him and shouted, "If you were my husband, I'd give you poison!"

"Madam," the umpire replied politely, "if I were your husband, I'd take it."

George Gershwin, pleased with himself, was once rhapsodizing about his latest musical score to some of his friends, among them dry-humored Oscar Levant.

Levant said nothing while Gershwin spoke. Then he asked, "George, if you had it to do over, would you fall in love with yourself again?"

Actor Will Rogers followed a pompous and long-winded speaker to the rostrum. The audience was almost asleep from boredom. But Rogers livened them up with a laugh when he announced, "You have just listened to that famous Chinese statesman, On Too Long."

A wild-eyed character who was convinced he was Napoleon burst into a psychiatrist's office, thrust his hand inside his coat, and declared, "It isn't myself I've come to see you about, Doctor. It's my wife Josephine. She thinks she's Mrs. Richardson."

A Broadway producer had lured a prospective backer to the theater to view an audition for his new musical. Sitting back in a front-row seat, the prospect watched each new female potential come out on the stage and display her charms, and muttered at each: "Phooey."

After six or seven beauties had crossed the stage, the producer lost patience and turned to his prospect. "What's the matter?" he barked. "Aren't these girls good enough for you?"

"Oh," the prospect replied, "I wasn't thinking of the girls at all."

"Then why do you keep saying 'phooey'?"

"I was thinking of my wife."

A mother tore into her son's bedroom and shook her son who was lying in bed. "Gerhardt," she said, "you've got to go to school. Enough of this nonsense, get up and go to school."

Gerhardt growled, "I don't want to go to school."

She shook him once again and said, "Gerhardt, I'm telling you, you've got to get up and go to school."

Gerhardt said, "Why?"

"Well," she yelled, "I'll give you three good reasons. In the first place, I pay taxes; in the second place, you're 50 years old; and in the third place, you're the principal."

The twenty-ninth President of the United States, Calvin Coolidge, was a reticent man, never known for scintillating conversation.

A socialite once sat next to him at a party and babbled, "Oh, Mr. President, do you know I made a bet today that I would get more than two words out of you?"

Maintaining his reserve, Coolidge responded quietly, "You lose."

# Black Jokes

Wallace dashed wildly into his apartment and found his wife in the kitchen. "Alice!" he gasped. "We've gotta move out of here right away. I just found out that the superintendent in this building makes love to every woman in it but one."

"Yeah, I know," his wife replied calmly. "That's that stuck-up thing on the fifth floor."

## Ain't It So!

A watch factory ran an ad for a precision man. The ad offered $100.00 per week. One guy answered the ad, filled out his application and asked for $200.00 a week.

The superintendent asked, "Have you ever worked in a precision factory before?"

The applicant answered, "No."

"And you have the nerve to ask for $200.00 a week?" bellowed the personnel director.

"Of course! said the jerk, "You know the work is much harder if you don't know how to do it."

A lawyer tried to discredit the witness. "You say that between the act that you described and the time he ran away, five minutes passed. Do you know exactly what five minutes are? Perhaps it was three minutes, or eight minutes, or two minutes? How do you have the nerve to say it was exactly five minutes?"

"Well," said the witness, "I tell you it was five minutes, and it was five minutes."

"Is that so?" said the lawyer, "I'll put you to the test. I have a watch right in front of me which I am laying down on the table. Now you tell me when five minutes have passed."

"Okay," said the witness.

At the end of five minutes, the witness cried out: "It's now five minutes."

The judge exclaimed, "The witness is correct."

The test so impressed the jury that they acquitted the defendant.

After the court was dismissed, the lawyer came over to the witness and said, "Well, you sure beat me, but I don't know how you did it. How did you do it?"

"Well," answered the witness affably, "I just figured it out."

"You figured it out; how did you do that?"

"Well, it wasn't hard. I just looked at the large clock which hung on the wall behind you."

## Man! Oh Man!

A man walked into an employment office to apply for a job. "What's your name?" the clerk asked him.

"Size-Six Holloway," the man replied.

"What kind of name is 'Size-Six'?" remarked the clerk.

"That really isn't my name," Halloway declared. "As a matter of fact, my name is "Six-And-Seven-Eighths!"

"I don't get you," said the bewildered clerk.

"Well, when I was born my parents didn't know what to name me," he explained, "so they put a few names in a hat. And my father accidentally pulled out the size of the hat."

## The Hustler

A census taker came up to a black sitting on a rocker in front of his cottage.

After the usual questions, the census taker said, "What kind of a business do you run?"

Mr. Cadwallader answered, "I own a hand laundry."

"You do?" asked the census taker, "where is it located?"

Back came the answer, "Here she comes now."

**A** jealous wife was searching her husband's pockets when she came across a card on which was scribbled, "Peggy Brown, Center 722." She confronted him with the card.

"Oh, that's nothing," her husband explained. "Peggy Brown is just the name of a race horse I bet on."

"Oh, yeah? Well then, what does this 'Center' mean?" she demanded.

"That's the name of the street where my bookmaker lives," he countered quickly.

"How about 722?" she challenged. "Get out of that one if you can!"

"Why dear, those are the odds—seven to two!" he said in hurt surprise.

His wife was forced to give up her interrogation.

But the following night when he came home he found his wife standing in the doorway.

"Anything new today, honey?" he asked.

"Oh, nothing much," she sneered, "except that your horse called up!"

## Practical Philosopher

Sam was hobbling down the street when he met up with his old friend Moe.

"What's wrong, Sam?" asked Moe. "Why are you hobbling so?"

"*Why*?" complained Sam loudly. "Because my shoes are absolutely killing me!"

Moe was confused. "So why do you wear them?" he asked.

"Well, I'll tell you," sighed Sam. "My business couldn't be worse. I owe the butcher, the baker, the grocer, the landlord. I have two daughters so ugly who knows if I'll ever be able to get them married. My son is a slob, and my wife nags, nags, nags until I go crazy. I come home each night from a lousy day's work, and I look at the bills and at my family, and at that point I could kill myself.

"So I take off these damned shoes—and, Moe, that's the only pleasure I ever get!"

**A** Southerner had hired Clem Johnson to cut a few cords of wood. When he came to oversee the work, he found Clem sitting by on a stump very comfortably, watching Bill Williams do the job.

"Clem, I hired you to cut that wood. How is it that I find Bill doing the job?"

"Don't you worry," answered Clem, "I'm going to pay Bill $3 to do that job."

"My!" exclaimed the white man, "I'm only paying you $2 to do the cutting."

"Yes sir, I know that, but it's worth a dollar to me just to be boss for once."

During an income tax examination, a black was asked how it was that after he had sold crops for $60,000 he showed no profit.

"Well," he countered, "the ducks got it."

"Oh," exploded the income tax agent, "the ducks got it. Who do you think you're kidding?"

"No sir," the black said. "I am telling the truth, the ducks got most of it."

"How do you explain that?" persisted the agent.

"Well, look here," continued the farmer. "I sent my crops to Chattanooga, and the railways *deducts* part of my money for shipping. Then they *deducts* another sum for handling. And when they come to send my check back, they *deducts* still more as a percentage of my sale. In fact, when it's all over, I got hardly any money at all. You see *de ducks* got most of it."

## Biblical Scholar

A minister was assailed by a teetotaling preacher for his liberal views about drinking.

The minister countered by replying, "There are two drinks mentioned in the Bible: wine: *which gladdeneth the heart of man,* and water: *which quencheth the thirst of the jackasses.*"

## Cheapskate

To start a small Christmas Club for his wife, Miller agreed to give her fifty cents every time she favored him. Mrs. Miller always dropped the coins into a small piggy bank she kept in her closet.

At Christmas the bank was opened, and Miller was shocked to see a number of one, five, and ten dollar bills among the contents.

"Wait a minute," he told his wife, "I only gave you fifty cents each time. Where did these bills come from?"

"Well," his wife replied, "do you think everybody is as cheap as you?"

## No Hurry

Jacob Elmont had been convicted of a capital crime, and had been sentenced to die in the electric chair. On the day of the execution, the warden came to Jacob and said, "It's your last day on earth, and as warden, I am empowered to give you the best breakfast you ever had. Just tell me what you want."

"Thank you," answered Jake, "I'll just have two watermelons, that's all."

"Oh, I'm sorry," answered the warden, "watermelons aren't in season now."

"Well," answered Jacob, "I'm in no hurry. I can wait."

## Jurisprudence

A black was arraigned on a charge of stealing a chicken. He got himself a very sharp lawyer, who proceeded to prove that on the night of the theft his client was at home in bed with excruciating rheumatism, and furthermore that he never ate chicken at any time.

The legal arguments and the cross examination continued for a long time. Finally, after much deliberation, the judge decided to dismiss the case.

The judge called the defendant up to the bar and said, "Jim Langford, you are acquitted. You can go home now."

"Oh, fine," answered the defendant. "Does that mean I can keep the chicken?"

The preacher was admonishing Bill Jones, who had been nursing a grudge against Tom Wills for months, and took every opportunity to harass Tom.

"If your neighbor does you an injury, you are ordered to forgive it and forget it," said the preacher.

"Yes, Preacher, I admit that, and I do forget it. But I have a miserably bad memory, and I keep forgetting that I forgot it."

A man obviously three sheets to the wind staggered down the street and bumped into a woman of obvious respectability. "You horrible creature," she glowered. "You are the drunkest man I have ever seen."

The drunk turned slowly and said, "Lady, you're the ugliest woman I've ever seen! And that's worse, 'cause when I wake up tomorrow, I'm gonna be sober."

The director of a modeling agency was interviewing a young woman for a job. After the usual questions, he ogled her and asked, "Are you a virgin?"

"Yes," she replied coyly, "but I'm not a fanatic about it!"

## No Question About It

A young man was applying for a job in a big company.

"I'm sorry," said the personnel manager, "but the firm is overstaffed; we have more employees now than we really need."

"That's all right," replied the young man, undiscouraged, "the little bit of work I do wouldn't be noticed."

Business was lousy. Morris Ginsberg of Ginsberg's Catskill Resort was just about ready to give up the hotel business and try something new.

"But," as he told his niece, who was visiting him during her college vacation, "at my age it's not easy to get started again."

"Uncle Morris, there's nothing wrong with the hotel . . . except that you don't have customers. What you need is a gimmick to bring them in."

"A gimmick," he echoed, "maybe you're right. But what kind of gimmick?"

So they put their heads together and decided on a Wild West motif. Ginsberg spent the last of his savings redecorating the hotel to look like one he'd seen in a cowboy picture. To go with the new look, he renamed the hotel "Westward Ho." The crowning glory was a stagecoach which he bought cheap from his cousin, the movie producer.

When everything was all ready he told his black driver, Franklin, to ride the stagecoach down to the train station to look for prospective guests. "If we offer them a free ride to the Westward Ho—in a stagecoach no less—we're sure to attract customers!"

Franklin returned hours later with a stagecoach full of men. Ginsberg knew his luck had changed. Every time a train came in, Franklin was there to meet it; and every time he came back he brought dozens of customers. But all males!

Ginsberg was full of praise for his driver. "Franklin," he said, "I'm giving you a raise. What do you do that brings those men into our hotel?"

"Mr. Ginsberg," replied Franklin, "I don't do nothing special. I just point to that stagecoach and yell "This way to the Westward Ho House!"

## Fair's Fair

Joe said to his friend Willie, "Willie, lend me twenty dollars."

Willie took out his wallet and handed Joe a ten dollar bill.

"Willie," said Joe "I asked you for twenty."

"Yes, I know," said Willie. "This way you lose ten and I lose ten."

The wife was pleading her case before the divorce court judge. "All I'm asking, Your Honor, is that my husband leave me the way he found me."

"But lady," the judge replied, "that's impossible."

"Why impossible?" she persisted. "He found me a widow!"

## Premier Exhibit

A ragged panhandler stopped Calloway on the street and asked for some money for a meal. "I'll tell you what I'll do," Calloway told him, "I'll buy you a drink."

"I don't drink," said the panhandler.

"Well then, I'll buy you a couple of good cigars."

"I don't smoke," the panhandler replied. "I just want a little money for something to eat."

"I've got a good tip on a nag in the sixth race this afternoon," Calloway continued. "I'll put up the money, you can take the winnings. How about it?"

"But, sir, I don't gamble," protested the panhandler. "All I want is a little money for a bite to eat."

"I'll tell you what I'll do," Calloway responded. "I'll take you home with me for dinner. I want my wife to meet you because I want her to see what can happen to a man who doesn't drink, smoke or gamble."

**A** pretty young girl was rushed to the hospital for the delivery of her child. Her boyfriend, Jim, waited anxiously downstairs. The delivery was extremely long and painful.

When it was all over, the girl sighed and said: "If this is what married life is like, go downstairs and tell Jim our engagement is off!"

Diary of a black girl on a Caribbean Cruise:

Monday: Was invited to dine at the captain's table.

Tuesday: Spent the day with the captain.

Wednesday: Captain made ungentlemanly proposals to me.

Thursday: Captain said he'd sink the ship if I didn't agree to his proposals.

Friday: Saved 500 lives.

A father and his son were walking through the park, and every few steps the little boy would ask another question.

"What is lightning?"

"Why is the sky blue?"

"What makes trains run?" and so on.

To each question his father replied that he didn't know.

"Pop," the boy continued, "do you mind if I ask you all these questions?"

"Not at all, son. Keep right on asking. How else will you ever learn anything?"

## Ten Bucks Is Ten Bucks

A disgruntled litigant yelled out to the judge, "Go to hell."

The incensed magistrate promptly declared, "You're in contempt of court! That's going to cost you ten dollars a word. I fine you $30!"

Considerably chastened, the litigant thought it over and apologetically asked, "Your Honor, can I amend my remark to '*Fuck you.*'?"

## Pulling Rank

The cute one came to the doctor's office complaining she felt a burning sensation when she went to the bathroom.

"You've got P.D.," said the doctor.

"What's that?" she asked.

"Why, that's a private disease," answered the physician.

"That faker!" shouted the cutie. "He told me he was a lieutenant."

## Coming up in the World

The prosecutor was needling him something fierce. Bill Morgan squirmed in his chair. He knew he would have a hard time.

The prosecutor sneered as he said, "What do you do for a living?"

"I dig ditches," answered Bill.

"You do? Well, that's a high-toned profession."

"Well," retorted Bill, "I'm doing better than my father did."

"Is that so?" answered the prosecutor. "What did he do?"

"He was a shyster lawyer."

## Simple Enough!

Jasper Montgomery loved to gamble. But one day he had a terribly miserable day at the track. He complained to his brother, Danny, and said, "I don't know. When I play cards, I always win. But at the race track, I always lose. How can you explain it?"

"That's easy," replied his brother, "it's because you can't shuffle the horse."

**R**oberts became convinced he was a cannibal, and his wife finally persuaded him to visit a psychiatrist. When Roberts returned home after his first visit, his wife asked, "So tell me, what is a fancy psychiatrist like?"

"Delicious," beamed Roberts.

Little Sammy had decided that the only way to get ahead in the army was to act tough and throw his weight around. Two weeks after his arrival in boot camp, he stood in the middle of his barracks and loudly declared, "Show me a sergeant, and I'll show you a fool!"

His words were no sooner spoken when a six-foot-five sergeant appeared behind him. He glared down at little Sammy and bellowed, "I'm a sergeant!"

"Well, I'm a fool!" whispered Sammy

Joe Johnson applied for a job. The personnel manager told him there was only one job open, a very good one that paid $300 a week, and asked him if he wanted it.

"What is it?" asked Joe.

"It's a job to be the chief worrier for this company."

"I'll take it," said Joe, "but who pays me the $300?"

"That," said the personnel manager, "is your first worry."

## Psychologist

Moe went to a department store to buy himself a suit. He found just the style he wanted, so he took the jacket off the hanger and tried it on.

A salesman came up to him. "Yes, sir. It looks wonderful on you."

"It may *look* wonderful," said Moe irritably, "but it fits terrible. The shoulders pinch."

The salesman didn't bat an eye. "Put on the pants," he suggested. "They'll be so tight, you'll forget all about the shoulders!"

## Of Course Not!

Harry Robinson had just entered the parlor of a familiar bagnio when, to his utter shock, he spotted his own father coming down the stairs.

Harry reeled back in surprise. "Dad!" he cried out. "What in God's name are you doing in a place like this?"

Old Robinson was equally stunned, but quickly recovered. "Now, son," he said, nonchalantly brushing off his suit, "for twenty lousy bucks would you want me to bother your dear, hard-working mother?"

**A** crook gave his girl a beautiful fur coat. She paraded up and down admiring herself in the mirror, and then asked him "Chuck, darling, what's it worth?"

"Oh, from three to six years."

## What a Defense!

The man had been a menace. He had gone around town just slugging people right and left; and when he ran out of victims on the street, he came home and slugged his wife.

The judge stared down at him from his bench. "You know, the last time you were before me I told you that if you kept on with your miserable conduct I would put you away for a long stretch."

"Well," the man answered, "I know that and I kept it in mind, and I really behaved myself. One day about two weeks ago I was at home and my wife, Emelina, needles me and says, 'I know why you're so nice to me now. It's because you're afraid of that no-good, cheap judge, that's why.'

"Well, Your Honor, when she said that, I just got up and busted her one in the mouth."

**A** panhandler walked up to a well dressed man and said, "Mister, can you let me have five dollars?"

"What!' exclaimed the other. "Five dollars! You have some gall. Where do you get the nerve to ask me for five dollars?"

"Well," said the panhandler, "I just want to quit early today."

"Please let me have a dime," said the panhandler to a passing gentleman.

Twenty minutes later, he met the same man again and asked for another dime.

The pedestrian got angry. "You lousy bum," he said, "Didn't I give you a dime just twenty minutes ago?"

"Okay, okay," came back the answer, "Stop living in the past."

A couple went into a shopping mall, and left their kid in a baby carriage with the other parked baby carriages. On the way out, the father grabbed a baby carriage and turned it over to his wife.

A few blocks outside, she exclaimed, "Jim, this is not our child."

"Shut your big mouth," he replied, "this is a much better carriage."

A palooka was really being pushed around in the ring. His opponent swarmed all over him and gave him a terrible thrashing.

After the fight, the palooka talked to his manager in the dressing room: "Do you know I had him really worried in the sixth round—he thought he killed me."

It was in a Pullman. The traveler asked in the dining car for a piece of Washington Pie, which the menu featured.

When the dessert arrived, it was a black chocolate cake with chocolate sauce. The traveler complained. "I thought Washington Pie was a white cake with a white sauce."

"Well," answered the waiter, "in this country there are two Washingtons, and two Washington Pies. The one that you had in mind was a *George* Washington pie. That's white cake with white sauce. The pie we have on this here train is named after *Booker T.*"

Two black sociologists developed a project in college. They were going to get a cannibal and bring him up so that he would be fully civilized.

They gave him western clothes; they sent him to college; and they taught him the ways of civilized man.

When he got his degree, they gave him a present of a voyage on an ocean liner.

When the cannibal sat for his first sitting in the dining salon, the steward hovered over him and obsequiously murmured, "Would you like to see the menu?"

"No," the man said, "just the passenger list."

After a long vacation in Florida where they hired a black maid, the couple came back to their home in New Britain, Connecticut. Here the maid was taught how to handle a telephone call. She was told to find out first who was calling, then tell the caller to hold the wire, and then summon that member of the family who was wanted.

After a week, Sally, the maid, became terribly lonesome for Orlando, Florida. When the phone rang next, the operator said, "It's a long distance from Florida."

"You said it!" cried Sally, and hung up.

## Top Financier

He was earning $100 a week as a stock clerk, and yet he was sporting around the city in a Cadillac, had a country home, and a yacht. The boss could no longer control his outrage, and called him in and said, "Andrew Robinson, I earn $1,000 a week and I can't begin to live on the scale that you do. Where do you get that kind of money?"

"Well," answered Andy, "I run a raffle every week and I sell tickets for $1 apiece."

"A raffle, you say. What the hell do you raffle?"

Andrew answered, "My $100 salary check."

A passenger on a Pullman called the porter and said, "Say, Porter, you've given me the wrong pair of shoes. There's one black and one brown."

Sam scratched his head and said, "That's funny, that's the second time this morning this here thing has happened."

His hoity-toity wife tried to be intellectual. She would go to dance recitals, concerts, lectures, etc.

One night, she dragged him into Aeolian Hall to hear a recital, and he sat through the proceedings squirming all the time.

"They're playing Beethoven's Ninth Symphony," she said.

"And am I happy," he said, "that I missed the first eight."

An old black had been buying lottery tickets for years, and never won. The members of the lodge felt sorry for him, so when he said he chose No. 4, they decided to write No. 4 on all the tickets in the hat. They were going to make him a winner, no matter what.

The old black was blindfolded. He put his hand in the hat, fidgeted around, and then drew out No 7¼.

A smart Harlem merchant put a display of new evening dresses in his window, along with the following sign: "These dresses are built like a fence. They protect the property but do not obstruct the view."

Four of the boys were in love with Gloria. They all got down on their knees at the same time and proposed to her.

But Gloria would have none of them. She turned them all down.

So it wouldn't be a total loss, they remained on their knees and started a crap game.

Annabelle wasn't feeling well, and she knew she should see a doctor. So she asked her friend Lana the name of the doctor she used.

"His name's Feinstein," said Lana, "but he's expensive."

"How expensive?" asked Annabelle.

"Well, it's fifty dollars for the first visit, and twenty-five for every visit after that."

So Annabelle went off to see Dr. Feinstein. When her turn came to be examined, she smiled brightly and said to the nurse, "Hi, honey. Here I am again!"

Ethel lay in bed freezing; the draft from the open window ran icy cold through her blanket. But her husband Sam was snoring deeply, unaware of his spouse's discomfort.

Finally Ethel could take it no longer. She propped herself up on an elbow and poked a finger in her husband's stomach. "Sam, Sam, it's cold outside," she exhorted. "Sam, close the window." But Sam didn't move.

Ethel tried again. "Sam, *Sam!*" She shook her husband's shoulder. "Get up and close the window. It's cold outside!"

Now Sam awoke, somewhat furious. "So if I close the window," he growled, "will it be warm outside?"

## Sure Enough!

Said Josephine, "I'm very popular with men. I wonder why. It must be my figure."

"No," answered Bill, "it isn't your figure."

"Then it must be my eyes, or my hair, or my soft hands."

"No, Josephine."

"Then it must be my personality."

"No, it isn't your personality," answered Bill.

"Well," said Josephine, "I give up."

Bill said, "Yes, Josephine that's it!"

## Maybe!

Bill called up Danny, his pal, with a tale of woe. "I was out with a real terrific dame tonight. I took her to a top cafe, and I ordered a bottle of very expensive wine. As soon as she drank half the bottle, what do you know, she threw her arms around me and kissed me. And boy, what a time I had!"

"So what are you complaining about?"

"Because I think I could have gotten the same result on beer."

A panhandler approached an old lady, and said "Missus, I haven't eaten a thing in four days."

"You haven't?" said the old lady. "Why, you must force yourself."

Two horseplayers walked out of church. One admonished the other and said, "Jackie, the word is *Hallelujah*—not *Hialeah.*"

Big Jim Scott applied for a job as a hotel detective. Then, just as he was leaving, the hotel keeper noticed something. "Mr. Scott, I see you've only got one eye."

"Why, that's true, boss, but that's enough for a keyhole."

"I heard you had a fight with your wife last night. How did it wind up?"

"Not bad—she came crawling to me on her knees."

"Is that so? What did she say?"

"Come out from under that bed, you coward."

A beggar stopped a businessman and asked if he could spare a quarter.

The businessman drew himself up and asserted, "I don't hand out money on the street."

The beggar retaliated, "So what should I do? Open up an office?"

A black of unsavory reputation died. At the funeral the parson asked for someone who could say something nice about the deceased.

No one volunteered. No one could think of anything to say in the dead man's favor.

After continued insistence by the parson, one man stood up and said "His brother was worse."

# British Jokes

At an army welcoming party, the long-winded commanding general of the base was delivering a boring, self-congratulatory oration. A young second lieutenant, tired of standing, muttered to the woman at his side, "What a pompous old windbag that fool is."

The woman turned to him at once and barked, "Lieutenant, do you know who I am?"

"No, I don't, Ma'am."

"I am the *wife* of that 'pompous old windbag,' as you call him."

"Oh my!" the young lieutenant blanched. 'Do you know who I am?"

"No, I don't," said the general's wife.

"Thank God!" the lieutenant replied, slipping off into the crowd.

Rudyard Kipling once received an unusual letter from some students at Oxford University. Gossip had it that Kipling received a shilling a word for what he wrote. The students enclosed a shilling and requested, "Please send us one of your words."

Kipling's reply was prompt: "Thanks!"

The admiral was aboard his flagship in a Mediterranean port. The captain of one of the cruisers had made a very sloppy job of it when it was up to him to bring his ship into berth.

The captain knew he had made a foul-up, and dreaded the wrath of his commanding officer. Finally, the message came from the flagship. It was but one word, "Good."

Fifteen minutes later, the confused captain was startled by the delivery of another message from the admiral. It ran: "To previous message, please add the word 'God!'"

The duke woke up in a very manly condition. He summoned Jeeves.

"Ah," said Jeeves, when he saw what he hadn't seen in months. "Shall I summon the Duchess?"

"Oh, no!" said the Duke. "Just fetch me a pair of very baggy trousers. I'm going to try to smuggle this thing into London."

G.K. Chesterton was a man of ample proportions, whose brilliant humor and love for life made friends even of those who disagreed with his strong religious views.

On one occasion, meeting his friend

George Bernard Shaw, Chesterton gestured toward the playwright's slender frame and said, "Looking at you, Shaw, people would think there was a famine in England."

Eyeing the other's corpulent figure, Shaw replied, "And looking at you, Chesterton, people would think you were the cause of it."

## Quite Right

A tough top sergeant glared at the pint-sized rookie and shouted, "What's the first thing you do when you clean a rifle?"

The rookie replied in a low-pitched voice, "Look at the serial number."

"The serial number!" roared the sergeant, "Why look at the serial number?"

"To make sure," explained the rookie mildly, "that I'm cleaning my own rifle."

**T**he American soldier stood on a London street corner.

An English lass passed by, and a gust of wind lifted her dress higher than was decent.

"A bit airy," remarked the friendly soldier.

To which the Cockney gal retorted, "'Ell yes! What did you expect—feathers?"

Porter paced back and forth in the doctor's waiting room while his wife underwent a complete physical examination inside. Finally the doctor opened the door and summoned the husband. "To be blunt, Mr. Porter," he said gravely, "I don't like the looks of your wife."

"Neither do I," Porter responded, "but she's great with the kids."

Wilson urgently needed to know the time, but his wristwatch had stopped hours before. The only person in sight, moreover, was a man sunning himself in the fenced-in lawn of the local mental hospital.

Dubious but desperate, Wilson called out, "Sir, do you by any chance have the time?"

"The time? One moment." The man on the lawn sprung into action, leaping out of his chair and withdrawing a small stick from one pocket and a small hammer from another. He tapped the stick into the ground, adjusted it carefully, and then pulled out a measuring tape and measured the length of its shadow. Throwing himself on the ground, he sighted the top of the stick and made a mark on the ground, then made a few new measurements.

Out from his back pocket came a slide rule, then an electric calculator. He made a few more feverish calculations, and then, perspiring heavily, answered: "It is exactly 4:28 P.M., provided this is May 20, as I believe it is."

Wilson, who had watched all this with astonishment, was quite impressed, and adjusted his watch carefully. "This has been an impressive use of solar position to tell time," he told the stranger, "but what do you do on a cloudy day when there are no shadows to measure?"

"Oh, that's no problem," said the inmate, holding up his right arm. "I just look at my wristwatch."

## Obvious Distinction

The power of Benjamin Disraeli's wit was perhaps nowhere evidenced as keenly as in his long-standing antagonism with Parliamentarian William Gladstone.

Once, in a literary debate, Disraeli was asked if there was any differencce in usage between the words *misfortune* and *calamity.* He reflected for a moment, then said:

"There is a similarity, but there is also a profound difference. If, let us say, Mr. Gladstone were to fall into the Thames, that would be a misfortune. But if anyone were to pull him out, that would be a calamity."

## Prayer

The newlyweds had just moved into their first apartment, and had decided to begin married life with twin beds. During their first week in the apartment, the wife brought home and placed over her bed the motto: "I need thee every hour."

The husband promptly went out shopping and returned with a sign of his own, which read: "God give me strength."

## Take it easy, Merwin!

A father was walking through the park pushing his young son along in a baby carriage. The kid was howling uncontrollably. Everybody turned and stared.

The father merely kept repeating very softly, "Take it easy, Merwin. Take it easy. Control yourself."

A woman approached the distressed father. She said, "I am a teacher in a progressive school and I notice the way you handle your child. I must say that I admire the way you keep your temper. A fine looking lad you have in that carriage, Sir. So his name is Merwin."

"Oh, no," corrected the father. "His name is Oliver. *I* am Merwin!"

In the poorer section of London lived an elderly rabbi. He lived on the third floor of a tenement, and a sign at the building's entryway said, "Rabbi Goldberg Is Upstairs."

Much beloved by his congregation, he remained poor because he asked for nothing in return for his services. Anything he did receive, he gave to those needier than he.

Thus, when he died, the old rabbi had no money put aside to pay for his funeral. His congregation, however, scraped together what they could and gave him a simple burial. But they had no extra money for a headstone.

Instead, they took the sign that hung below at the rabbi's lodgings, and used it as a testament to the man for whom they felt such love and devotion. The sign still reads, "Rabbi Goldberg Is Upstairs."

A stylish lady entered a millinery shop and pointed out a hat in the window.

"That red one with the feathers and berries," she said. "Could you take it out of the window for me?"

"Certainly, madam," the clerk agreed. "I would be happy to."

"Thank you so very much," said the lady as she moved toward the exit. "The awful thing upsets me every time I pass by."

## Good Advice

A British navy admiral tells of the time his fleet was only fifteen minutes into practicing war maneuvers when one particularly inept lieutenant collided his ship with the admiral's.

The admiral knew it was the lieutenant's first command and that the young man was nervous; still, this was a serious error. He wired the lieutenant angrily, "What do you propose to do now?"

Meekly came the return signal, "Buy a small farm, sir."

## Service with a Smile

The debutante daughter of a wealthy family went off to a party and came home smashing drunk. She could hardly get herself up the stairs; the butler had to assist her. However, when he got her into her bedroom, she was so ossified that she couldn't get under the bedsheets, and he had to undress her and put her to bed.

The next morning, she had some dim recollection of the state she had been in, and the circumstances of the homecoming. She called the butler and said, "James, I don't remember much about last night except that you tried to give me some coffee which I couldn't down and that I couldn't get up the stairs. How did I come to wake up in bed?"

"Well," he answered, "you came home very tired, my lady."

But she pressed on. "James, I'm undressed and I'm in my nightgown."

"Well, I couldn't let you spoil your good evening clothes, my lady."

"Oh," she stammered, "do you mean that you undressed me and put me to bed without my knowing it? Tell the truth, was I tight?"

"Yes, my lady; but not after the first time."

John Wilkes, a member of Parliament during the last part of the 18th century, earned a reputation for free thinking and profligacy. Expelled from Parliament twice for libelous writings, Wilkes acquired many enemies during his tenure. On one occasion, his barbed wit was directed at a politician who had been insulted once too often.

"Sir," said his adversary, "I predict you will die either on the gallows or of some loathsome disease."

Wilkes shot back: "Which it will be, my dear sir, will depend entirely upon whether I embrace your principles or your mistress."

The Duchess of Marlboro was visiting a wounded captain at a military hospital. He had been accidentally shot in target practice.

The Duchess asked the officer, "Sir, just where were you wounded?"

The captain squirmed for a moment and then said, "I'm sorry, Madam, but I'd rather not discuss this delicate matter."

"Tut-tut," said the Duchess, "I've been married now for 15 years."

Not wanting to be rude, the captain replied, "I was shot in the penis."

The Duchess continued, "Was the bone broken?"

The officer sat bolt upright in bed, bowed slightly and remarked, "Fifteen years married, you say. Duchess, my compliments to the Duke."

A parson sauntered into his golf club one weekday morning. He wanted to play a round of golf, but nobody familiar was in sight. The only other person in the locker room was a stranger.

The parson approached him and said, "Are you looking for a game?"

"Yes. I'd be glad to play with you. But I always play for $10.00 a round."

The parson realized he wasn't much of a

golfer, but he was willing to pay $10.00 for the morning's pleasure and exercise, so he agreed.

Out on the links, the stranger took every unfair advantage. When the parson was putting, he'd start to jabber away. He cheated whenever he could, and he made the day miserable.

After the parson had paid off, he turned to the stranger and said, "Here's my card. Come to my church any Sunday. I'll be glad to see you, and give you my greetings. And you might bring along your parents, too. I'd like to meet them."

"Bring along my father and mother? Why?"

"Because then," rejoined the parson, "I could marry them."

A self-made man by the name of Bates managed to get his son into a posh college. At the beginning of the term, the student's family was invited to meet the dean.

Upon being presented to the guest of honor, the tycoon announced: "This is my wife, Mrs. Bates, and this is my daughter, Miss Bates, and my son, Master Bates."

"Does he?" replied the dean. "Well, we'll soon cure him of that."

**A** would-be poet approached a well-known professor of literature and asked if the man would take five minutes to look at some of his work.

The professor agreed, but when he began reading the poetry, a frown appeared on his brow.

"Do you think I ought to put more fire into my poetry?" asked the writer.

"Not at all," said the professor, handing the sheaf of papers back. "Just put more of your poetry into the fire."

## Quite Appropriate

An officer in the British Army was once court-martialed for being found totally undressed and chasing a young lady clad in a nightgown down a hotel corridor.

At the trial, however, he was set free due to a newly interpreted section of the army rules book: "It is not compulsory for an officer to wear a uniform at all times, as long as he is suitably garbed for the sport in which he is engaged."

**R**ugby:

*A game played by men with peculiarly shaped balls.*

The motorcycle siren screamed out. The sedan stopped. The cop pulled up to the figure at the wheel and bellowed, "I am arresting you on four counts. In the first place, you drove through a red light. In the second place, you're going the wrong way on a one-way street. In the third place, you have been tearing through the center of town at 60 miles an hour. And in the fourth place, you didn't slow down or stop though you heard my siren for the last ten blocks."

The driver's wife leaned across her husband and smiled at the cop.

"You mustn't be angry at him," she cooed, "he's dead drunk."

A chap was rowing down the Thames one Sunday when he lost one of his oars, and he drifted out to midstream. He tried to paddle with the one that remained but found the going difficult.

Just then, he noticed a boat coming downstream, in which sat a man and two women, all three rowing.

"I say," he shouted across the water, "lend me one of your oars."

The Cockney looked up indignantly "They're not 'ores!" he protested. "They're me mother and sister!"

In his early years in Parliament, Winston Churchill once decided it would be appropriate to print copies of his speeches and have them given to all the members of the House of Commons.

Entertained by the pompous gesture, the member for Devonshire sent Churchill this note:

"Dear Mr. Churchill. Thanks for the copy of your speeches lately delivered in the House of Commons. To quote the late Lord Beaconsfield: 'I shall lose no time in reading them.'"

## Noblesse Oblige

An American had been visiting at the castle of a member of the British peerage. As was usual in such castles, the rooms were enormous, the furniture grandiose, but the plumbing facilities were pitifully meager.

One morning, the American got up, bleary-eyed, to search for the one small bathroom he was told existed on the immense floor. He finally stumbled into a room in which the duchess was taking a bath, and he encountered her ladyship in all her nudity. With an embarrassed, "Beg pardon," the American bolted out of the room.

Fearing he might be considered less than a gentleman unless *he* reported the incident, he hastily dressed and went to his host's study, and recounted the happening in full to the duke.

The duke listened without moving a muscle. Then his lordship remarked, "Skinny bitch, isn't she?"

A very well-dressed woman entered a London cab. When she arrived at a certain department store, she asked the cabbie to wait for a moment; she'd be out very shortly. In fact, she had him leave the meter running.

The cabbie waited five minutes, ten minutes, and then half an hour, but the lady never reappeared.

So the cabbie got out of his cab, opened the back door, looked inside and—to his horror—discovered a big pile of freshly dropped shit on the seat.

Full of rage, he drove around to the London Constabulary, ran up to the officer at the desk, and blurted out, "And she called herself a lady, sir. Looked like a lady, too! And look what she left in my cab!"

"Don't have time for that!" answered the lieutenant impatiently. "Whatever the lady left, take it to Whitechapel, leave it there for 30 days, and then, if nobody claims it, it's yours!"

## British Syntax

An American girl visiting England was invited to a party. While dancing with a rather stuffy Briton, her necklace became unfastened and slipped down the back of her dress. She asked the Englishman to retrieve the jewelry for her.

He was very embarrassed. Yet wishing to comply with her request, he reached cautiously down the back of her gown.

"I'm terribly sorry," he said, "but I can't seem to reach it."

"Try further down," she said.

At this point, he noticed he was being watched by everyone in the room. He whispered to the girl, "I feel a perfect ass."

"Never mind that!" she replied. "Just get the necklace."

## Tom is at the Door!

The nouveau rich lady was giving a dinner. Everything seemed to be going fine, but she had a terrible cold, and her nose was running something awful.

She turned to her butler and said, "Williams, I just can't do anything about this nose of mine. I can't even feel when it's running. Please give me a hint so I don't become embarrassed. Just call out, "Tom is at the door," and then I'll know."

A few times when her nose was especially active, the butler called out, "Tom is at the door," and the lady took out her handkerchief and wiped away the secretion.

Toward the end of the meal, she became involved in an animated conversation. When the butler called out, "Tom is at the door," she didn't hear him and kept jabbering away. The butler cried out again, "Tom is at the door." But she was much too involved to listen.

In a couple of minutes she turned to the butler and asked, "What was it you said?"

The butler replied, "I said "Tom is at the door." But never mind now, it's too late. Tom is in the tea!"

The building site was a 30-story skyscraper. Timothy Clancy, the hodcarrier, lost his footing, and hurtling down into space he landed on his cranium. He went through the cement pavement like a shot, and finished up in the cellar.

His mates rushed down, expecting to shovel up the pieces, but there was Clancy rubbing his head and chuckling as he said to his friends, "Thank the good Lord for that concrete pavement. It broke my fall."

Lord Throttletown came home unexpectedly from grouse shooting to find the duchess in bed with a neighboring member of the landed gentry. Hot with anger, Throttletown summoned his butler and demanded his pistol.

The butler dutifully obeyed, and handed the weapon to the seething duke. The duke carefully took aim at the adulterer, but the butler interrupted the shot, advising, "Do the sporting thing, my lord. Shoot him on the rise, I say."

Sir Leslie Hoare-Belisha was a British government offical of high station. One day, he ran across an opponent who wished him no good.

After some meaningless chatter about proposed changes in a pending bill, the opposition man said, "Okay, Sir Leslie, we'll think about it; and when you get home, please give my regards to Mrs. W."

In 17th century England, the Church was an important part of family life. In the small villages, the minister was personally acquainted with every member of his congregation and with their problems.

Thus it was natural that, one Sunday in

Shropshire, Mrs. Whitfield wanted her pastor to mention Mr. Whitfield in the morning's prayers. Her husband had joined the Navy and was presently serving His Majesty, the King.

The lady sent a handwritten message to the pulpit: "Timothy Whitfield, having gone to sea, his wife desires the prayers of the congregation for his safety."

The aging preacher, however, had trouble reading the scrawled note. Without thinking, he quickly pronounced: "Timothy Whitfield, having gone to see his wife, desires the prayers of the congregation for his safety."

"Doctor," a man confessed to his psychiatrist, "I'm afraid that I'm in love with a horse."

"Is it male or female?" the doctor asked.

"Female, of course," the man snapped back. "What do you think I am, a queer?"

A fashionable customer came in to a hatter in Piccadilly. The obsequious clerk bowed low and said, "What's your pleasure?"

The gentleman answered, "Blondes. But the fact is I came in for a felt hat."

Professor Atkinson was a scientist. In fact, he was deemed to be the leading authority on zoological nomenclature.

One day, one of his assistants came running up to him, visibly upset. In an excited voice he cried out, "Professor Atkinson, something awful has just happened. Your wife has been swallowed by an alligator."

Atkinson looked up and said, "My man, you mean a crocodile."

An Englishman visiting America attended a banquet and heard the Master of Ceremonies give the following toast:

"*Here's to the happiest moments of my life. Spent in the arms of another man's wife—my mother.*"

"By jove, that's ripping," the Englishman thought to himself. "I must remember to use it back home."

Some weeks later when he returned to England, he attended a church luncheon and was asked to give a toast. In thunderous tones he addressed the crowded room:

"*Here's to the happiest moments of my life. Spent in the arms of another man's wife—*" And he stopped, deep in thought.

After a long pause the crowd began to grow restless, glaring at the speaker indignantly. The speaker's friend sitting next to him whispered, "You had better explain yourself quickly."

"By jove," the speaker blurted out, "You will have to excuse me. I forgot the name of the bloomin' woman."

"I'm afraid I've developed a terrible habit," the patient told his psychiatrist. "Wherever I am, I can't help talking to myself. Is there anything you can do for me?"

"I suppose there is," the psychiatrist replied. "But I should warn you it will be a long, slow, painful treatment, and very expensive as well. But suppose you do talk to yourself. Is that so bad?"

"No, I guess it isn't," the patient agreed. "But I'm *such* a bore."

In a rush-hour underground train, a gentleman bent over and murmured to the young lady standing beside him, "I beg your pardon, but would you like me to find a strap for you?"

"I have a strap," she retorted icily.

"Then please let go of my necktie!"

George Bernard Shaw's writing made sharp points with which not everyone agreed. Shaw was proud of his general acclaim, but he learned early to deal with his critics.

On opening night, one of his new plays was greeted with such favor that the audience called for him to take a bow. Suffused with pride, Shaw took several. But then one rowdy member of the audience called out loudly, "Shaw, your play stinks!"

The audience held its breath in horror. Shaw hesitated briefly, then said, "My friend, I agree with you completely. But what are we two against this great majority?"

In the midst of a geography lesson, the teacher noticed young Joey doodling on his desk. She asked him to stand. "Joey, what do you know about the Rumanian border?"

Startled, Joey blurted out, "Only that he goes out with my aunt, and my father doesn't like it!"

A male customer in a restaurant asked the waitress, "Where can I take a leak?"

She answered: "Just walk down this aisle and turn to the left. You'll see a door marked 'Gentlemen.' Pay no attention to the sign, and walk right in."

A vendor standing on the street offered cigars at 10 pence apiece. A man purchased one, lit the cigar, took a puff, and then began to cough violently.

"What kind of rot are you selling me?" he yelled, "this cigar is positively putrid!"

The vendor looked at him sympathetically, then pointed to three cases of merchandise lying next to him: "You're complaining! You only bought one! *Look at all I bought!*"

Mr. MacDonald's son said to him, "Can I please have a shilling, Dad?" "A shilling! What on earth for?" was the astonished reply.

"Well," explained the youngster, "there's a great big snake they're showing at the circus, and I'd like to see it."

"Here's a magnifying glass, son; go out and look at a work," was the instant response.

## It's the Same the Whole World Over

The big Texan had been boasting, "Why in Texas," he said, "you can get on a train, ride for six days, and you will still be in Texas."

The Englishman observed, "Why, that can happen here, too. We have the same trouble with our slow trains."

A self-made man was arguing with his son's college professor about the value of education. He thought an education was all right for his son, who wanted to become a doctor, but he believed a liberal education was a waste for anybody else. He was glad he had never seen the inside of a college classroom.

"Do I understand, sir," asked the professor, "that you are thankful for your ignorance?"

"Well, yes," boomed the father, "you can put it that way if you wish!"

"Well, then, all I have to say is that you have much to be thankful for."

A Britisher was traveling in the remoter sections of Ireland. He stopped at an inn and asked the owner to serve him a whiskey.

The owner apologized and said, "I'm so sorry, but we have licensing rules in this part of the country, and we only open the bar at 11:00 a.m. It's ten o'clock now. Would you mind waiting?"

"No," answered the Britisher. "I would be glad to take advantage of your hospitality." And he sat himself down.

A few minutes later, the Irishman approached him and said, "It's a full hour's wait. While you're sitting and waiting, would you have a drink of Scotch?"

Sir C. Aubrey Smith entered his favorite posh restaurant and was ushered to his customary corner for a tranquil dinner. Unfortunately, his peace was disturbed when a dissatisfied patron at the next table began complaining loudly.

"What do you have to do to get a glass of water in this dump?" shouted the man.

Irritated, but maintaining his equanimity, Sir Aubrey leaned over and suggested, "Why don't you try setting yourself on fire?"

An adolescent once asked his librarian mother, "If you were shipwrecked, alone on a distant island, and could have one book, which one would you choose?"

The mother didn't even think twice. "*Johnson's Manual of Ship Building!*" she said.

Before the dinner guests began to arrive, the hostess cautioned her new maid: "Remember to serve from the left of each guest, and to clear the dishes away from the right. Understand?"

"Yes, Ma'am," replied the maid. "Are you superstitious or something?"

One Shakespearean actor was approached by a critic after a performance. "Tell me," said the critic, "do you think Shakespeare intended us to understand that Hamlet had relations with Ophelia?"

"I don't know what Shakespeare intended," said the actor. "Anyway, I always do."

After bargaining for hours, Witherspoon and his client finally approached an agreement. Witherspoon studied the client's latest offer, then pressed the intercom to talk to the bookkeeper. "Miss Holly," he yelled, pencil poised in hand, "if someone offered you $6,000 less 8%, how much would you take off?"

The voice came back immediately: "Everything but my earrings!"

A guard from a lunatic asylum rushed up to a pedestrian and said, "I'm looking for an escaped lunatic. Did you see him pass by?"

"What does he look like?" asked the man.

"He's very short, he's very thin, and he weighs about 325 pounds."

"What?" asked the man, "How can a man be short and thin and still weigh 325 pounds?"

"Well," said the guard angrily, "I told you he was crazy."

# Canadian Jokes

A well-dressed gentleman walked into a tavern, demanded a double shot of Scotch, downed it in one gulp, tossed a five-dollar bill on the bar, and walked out without saying a word.

The bartender picked up the bill and put it in his pocket. "How do you like that? The guy comes in here, downs a double Scotch, leaves a five-dollar tip, and then runs off without paying!"

Cyril, a plumber, died. His union called a meeting to raise money for his bereft, poverty-stricken wife and children. Contributions were to be voluntary.

One of the union members got up and made such a stirring speech that half the men started to weep and sob out loud. There wasn't a dry eye in the congregation.

But one man sat there unmoved, with not a trace of emotion showing on his face. His neighbor turned to him and said, "How come you're not crying?"

"I'm not a member here," was the answer.

"Fixation," remarked Dr. Zeekel, a noted psychiatrist, "can be compared to the case of the Montreal drunk who kept muttering, 'It can't be done! It can't be done! It can't be done!' as he stood looking up at a big electric sign that read, 'Drink Canada Dry.'"

## Panadian Holiday

A businessman was on holiday in Canada. He decided to take advantage of the fine lake at his camp, so he wired his secretary in Rochester: "Send up two punts and a canoe."

His dutiful secretary wired back: "The girls are on their way, but what the hell is a 'panoe'?"

## Tell It Like It Is

A man and his wife were celebrating their 50th wedding anniversary. They invited their two sons to the celebration, but neither of them showed up. They didn't even bother to send a gift or a congratulatory message.

About a month later, the sons paid the old couple a visit and were treated to a sumptuous dinner. They offered the weakest excuses for their failure to attend the Golden Wedding celebration. One of the sons claimed that he was out of town on a business trip, and the other said that he was involved in a golf tournament.

The father and mother were more depressed than impressed. Suddenly, the old man announced, "Boys, I have something to tell you that I've never told you before. The fact is, that although we celebrated our 50th wedding anniversary, your mother and I were never really married."

"What?" shrieked one of his sons, "What you're telling us that we're bastards!"

"That's right!" asserted the father, "And cheap ones, too!"

## Period

Mrs. Diamond had wheedled some money from her husband to have the house redecorated, and she hired an interior designer to help do the job.

"All right," said the decorator, "now how would you like it done? Modern?"

"Me, modern? No." said Mrs. Diamond.

"How about French?" suggested the decorator.

"*French*? Where would I come to have a French house?"

"Perhaps Italian provincial?"

"God forbid!"

"Well, madam, what period *do* you want?"

"What period? I want my friends to walk in, take one look, and drop dead! Period!"

A young boy and girl entered the movie theater and took seats just in back of an old biddy. After a few minutes, the girl began to giggle. In fact, she kept on giggling for some time.

The old biddy couldn't stand it any longer. Finally, she turned to the girl and said, "Young lady, are you feeling hysterical?"

The girl giggled a little more and replied, "No, ma'am, he's feeling mine."

The town was in an uproar. An inmate of the local lunatic asylum had escaped and had raped two women. Everybody was horrified.

Late that afternoon, the local newspaper's headline ran: nut bolts and screws.

Psychologist: Do you cheat on your wife?

Patient: On who else?

The lady told the psychiatrist, "My husband thinks I'm crazy just because I like pancakes."

"But there's nothing wrong with that," said the doctor. "I like pancakes myself."

"Do you?" cried the lady in delight. "Then you must come up some time. I have six trunks full."

His home was in Toronto; in fact, right on the border between the United States and Canada. That particular border had been in dispute for a number of years, but finally the Commission came to a decision, and he was advised that his house was situated in the United States.

"Oh, what a relief! Now I don't have to go through those terrible Canadian winters any more."

A traveling salesman walked into a hashery. He instructed the waitress, "Look, I want two eggs, and I want them fried very hard. I want two pieces of toast burnt to a crisp, and I want a cup of coffee weak, luke warm, and practically undrinkable."

"What!" exclaimed the waitress, "What kind of an order is that?"

"Never you mind," insisted the salesman, "just bring me what I asked for."

The waitress went back to the kitchen; told the chef there was a looney guy outside and gave him the order. The chef prepared everything just as it was ordered. The waitress brought the miserable breakfast back to the table, and said coolly, "Anything else, Sir?"

"Why, yes," said the salesman, "please sit down next to me and nag me. I'm feeling homesick."

An army lieutenant asked his superior, Captain Smith, to reprimand a private who spent his free time teaching the other men the art of gambling. The captain was a sober, moral man, and if anyone could straighten Jones out, he could.

Private Jones entered Captain Smith's quarters with a neatly pressed uniform, newly shined shoes, and a smart salute.

"At ease, young man," began Captain Smith. "Now, is it true that you're a gambler?"

"Sir," answered Jones respectfully, "it's a habit I just can't seem to lose. Why, I'll bet you ten dollars right now that you have a mole on your left shoulder."

The captain saw this as a chance to make a point. He knew Private Jones rarely lost a bet, but he also knew he had no mole. If he could force the private to lose, he might be able to reform him. Laying down the ten dollars, he stripped off his shirt and pointed to his smooth left shoulder.

"See there, young man? No mole," Smith asserted. "Let that be a lesson to you. Gambling simply does not pay." Private Jones stared at his shoes dolefully, and after being dismissed, went back to his barracks.

Captain Smith immediately called in the lieutenant and told him what had happened.

Puffed up with pride, he couldn't understand the lieutenant's silence. "What's the matter?" Smith asked finally. "Aren't you pleased?"

"No, sir," the lieutenant said slowly. "You see, on the way to your quarters Jones bet me twenty-five dollars he'd have the shirt off your back in five minutes."

## Hard to Take

A student went to consult his former professor of philosophy about a problem. When he arrived at the professor's home, he found him in front of the house, building a concrete sidewalk.

The student began to present his problem, but the professor interrupted him again and again by explaining to him what a thrill it was to build a sidewalk with his own hands.

As they were chatting, two young boys ran out of a driveway and stomped right through the freshly poured cement. The professor picked up a shovel and chased the boys down the street, cursing vehemently.

The student was aghast at the professor's emotional display. When the professor returned, the student remarked, "Why, Professor, I thought you liked children!"

The professor replied, "In the abstract, yes—but in the concrete, no!"

A couple received two tickets in the mail for a hit show. No name identified the donor.

They thought some of their friends might be sending them a gift; so they called a few but all denied they had been the donors.

Maybe the theater had sent the tickets by mistake. "No," said the box office, "but if nobody asks for them by 8:15 p.m. you can use them."

On the night of the performance they stood in the theater lobby and waited and wondered. At 8:30 they went in to see the show. They enjoyed themselves immensely and kept wondering how they got those great seats.

When they came home all the furniture was upset, things were scattered all over the place, and all the silverware was gone. On the dining table a note read, "No you know from whom."

Two young fellows were in a business that wasn't doing so well. One day one of them came to his partner and said, "I was walking down the street and passed that fancy shoe shop on 12th Street, and would you believe it, they had only one pair of shoes in the window—just one pair of shoes. But that pair of shoes were alligator shoes, and they were asking $330 for the pair. There must be a fortune in that business."

"Yes," said his partner, Tom. "There must be, and if we're to get alligator shoes, we'll have to go to Africa, that is, one of us will have to go."

It was decided that Bill should go, and they scraped together all their money to buy the ticket.

Bill was gone two months, and his partner Tom still didn't hear from him. Getting itchy, Tom flew over to Africa and found his partner on the banks of a stream on which were piled 15 alligator hides.

And there in the water stood Bill knee-deep, wrestling with a huge alligator. He spied Tom, and said, "I tell you, Tom, if this son-of-a-bitch doesn't have shoes on, I'm going to call it quits and go home."

All the girls from the office poured into a crowded cafeteria for the coffee break. One of the girls lit a cigarette and blew ring after ring of smoke.

An elderly lady, sitting next to her, was supremely annoyed. "Miss," she said, "that smoking is a horrible habit. I would rather commit adultery than smoke."

"So would I," answered the girl, "but, there just isn't time during a coffee break."

One bright youngster was being paraded before a guest to demonstrate his precocity. The guest, who was a history teacher, said to the boy:

"Well, now, young man, do you know what contributions the Phoenicians made to history?"

"Blinds," promptly answered the wide-eyed child.

Reverend McTavish had just been shown to his room in a Toronto hotel. The bellboy had dragged up two of his heavy suitcases. Reverend McTavish thanked the bellhop, who then stood waiting for a tip.

"Haven't you forgotten something, Reverend? You know it's customary to give a gratuity."

Reverend McTavish looked the bellhop straight in the eye and said, "I don't have any money, but tell me now, are you a drinking man?"

The bellhop's eyes brightened, and he said "Yes, I am."

"Well, then," continued McTavish, "as a gratuity for your services, you kneel down in front of me, and I will have you take the temperance pledge."

# Chinese Jokes

A very rich Chinese man owned a restaurant that was doing quite well; more and more customers poured in daily, and profits rose steadily.

But one thing irritated him. Next door, there lived a poverty-stricken countryman whose tiny Chinese laundry gave him but a paltry income. The restaurant owner knew that the laundryman was so poor that all he had to eat was rice, and he also knew that the unfortunate man had set his dining table up near the restaurant so that while he ate his rice he could smell the delicious aromas of the cooking next door.

The wealthy Chinese man was not unhappy that his brother did not eat well, but only that he received something for nothing by living so close to the fragrances of his restaurant. So one day he decided to send the poor man a bill for the smell of his food.

The poor laundryman came to visit the next day with the bill in one hand and his money box in the other. He rattled the coins in the restaurant owner's ear, then said, "I hereby pay for the smell of your food with the sound of my money."

A Chinese went to a broker's office with a certified check for $100,000 in his pocket. He told the stockbroker to invest the money for him in the stock market. "You choose any stock you wish. I trust you," said the Oriental. He received a receipt for his money. In two weeks, the Chinese came back to ask his financial counselor how things were going.

"Ah," said the other, "I'm sorry to say that the condition of the market during the past two weeks has been rather soft. As a matter of fact, due to fluctuation in the overseas money market, your stocks have receded somewhat. I must ask you to give me $5,000 more to cover your shrunken investment."

The Chinese answered, "Okay. I send you check for $5,000 tomorrow morning."

Another three weeks passed, and the Chinese came in again. "Tell me, how things?" he asked.

"A bit disturbing," answered the stockbroker. "Due to severe fluctuations, the market has plummeted again. I'm afraid we'll need another $15,000 to cover your investment."

And the Chinese plunked down another fifteen grand.

One month later, the investor came in to see his broker. When the broker saw him, woe spread across his face. The Chinese took one look and understood.

"Flucked again?" he asked.

**A** man walked into a Chinese restaurant and asked, "What's the specialty today?"

The answer was "Pizza Pie."

"What? This is a Chinese restaurant, isn't it? You have Italian pizza pie?"

"Yes, this is a Jewish neighborhood."

**W**ellington Koo was in the United States to represent China at the Washington Conference in 1921. In those pre-United Nations days, even urbane Washingtonians were not used to foreigners on their soil, and Koo found that people did not know quite how to approach him.

One socialite he sat next to at a dinner party turned to him after some time and brightly asked, "Likee soupee?"

Koo was tired of explanations and apologies, so he just smiled and nodded and continued with his dinner. When the meal ended, Koo was invited to say a few words to the guests. He agreed and spoke for twenty minutes in flawless English.

In his seat again, he noticed his condescending neighbor had blushed deep red and was now silent. With equanimity, Koo turned to her and asked, "Likee speechee?"

Near an air base, a Chinese walked into a saloon and met a group of American flyers. He told them he had been in the Chinese air force.

One of the Americans asked him what his name was, and he replied "Chow Mein."

Then another asked him what he did in the Chinese air force. He said, "Well, I was a Kamikaze flyer."

"Hold on," said one of the Americans. "If you were really one of those Kamikaze flyers, you wouldn't be here now to tell the tale. A Kamikaze would have plunged his plane in a suicide dive."

"Oh, yes," the Chinese replied, "Me Chicken Chow Mein."

A Britisher went to the cemetery to pay his respects to an old friend. He brought with him a small wreath of flowers.

At the gravesite, the Englishman gave several moments to the memory of his friend, then looked up to see a Chinese man at a grave several yards ahead. The Oriental was just rising after depositing a bowl of rice on the grave.

Amused, the Britisher called out, "What time do you expect your friend to come up and eat the rice?"

The Chinese gentleman bowed politely, then shouted back, "At about the same time your friend comes up to smell the flowers."

# French Jokes

**A** man came into a smart restaurant. He was shown to a fine table, sat down, and ordered *Salad Niçoise, Chicken Marengo, Perdi a la Brettone, Pheasant under Glass,* and wound up with *Crepes Suzettes, Demi-Tasse, Napoleon Brandy,* and a three dollar cigar. All during the meal, he ordered a different wine with every course.

When he finished, he asked to see the manager. The manager came over, and the customer said, "Do you remember that just about a year ago I came in here and ordered a sumptuous dinner just like this one. I couldn't pay for it, and you kicked me out into the street just like a dirty dog."

The manager thought for a moment, and said, "Yes, I'm sorry about that, but I remember it."

"Well, then," said the customer, "I'll have to trouble you again."

**M**ax sat in a restaurant waiting for his meal. He tapped a passing waiter on the arm. "Excuse me, what time is it?"

"Sorry," came the reply, "Where you're sitting is not my table."

## Tanked Up for Tiger

It happened in Africa. A Legionnaire had been condemned to death. However, the Sultan was in an indulgent frame of mind. When the prisoner was brought before him, his Majesty declared: "I'm going to give you a chance for your life. Before us, there stand three tents. In each tent, there is an almost superhuman task to perform. If you succeed in all three tents, I'll pardon you.

In the first tent is a gallon of wine: you must drink it all down within 15 minutes.

In the second tent is a ferocious tiger, suffering from a horrible toothache. You must extract the tooth in 15 minutes.

In the third tent, there is a powerfully built Amazonian virgin, who has resisted the advances of the strongest men in my realm. You cannot overpower her, but you have 15 minutes to seduce her."

The prisoner thanked the Sultan for being given a chance to live, and then proceeded to the first tent.

In 10 minutes, he emerged staggeringly drunk, holding upside-down an empty wine jug in one hand. On unsteady feet, he plunged into the second tent.

Seconds later, everyone's blood curdled because of the terrible screams and roars which came forth from that tent. About eight minutes later, the prisoner emerged from the second tent, a horrible bloody mess, covered with long scratches, deep bites, and fearful gouges from the tiger's claws. To look at him was sickening.

Reeling up to one of the royal attendants, the prisoner demanded: "Now where's the girl with the toothache?"

An American in Paris asked a cabby to give him the address of a good brothel. He went there alone, selected his partner, and ordered dinner. Later that evening, after having satisfied his every whim, the thoroughly drained gentleman went downstairs and asked the madam for his bill.

"There is no charge, Monsieur," said the lady of the house.

Astonished, but not disposed to argue the matter, the gentleman departed.

The next night he returned to the brothel and repeated his performance of the previous night. Upon leaving this time, however, he was shocked to learn that his bill was 800 francs.

"Impossible!" the American shrieked. "I was here last evening and I got everything, and you didn't charge me a sou!"

"Ah," said the madam, "but last night you were on television!"

A Parisian impresario announced that a sensational show would be shown in a Montmartre hall. He would produce an incredible young man who would screw 10—yes, 10 women—in one hour.

The hall was packed. All tickets had been sold. On the stage were 10 beds side by side, with a pretty girl on each one of them.

The young man stepped forth to great applause, flexed his muscles, and then sprang into the first bed. It took him but two minutes to do the job, and then he leaped into the second bed.

He did his thing, and then went to the third bed. The audience was in rapt attention. Then the incredible man serviced the fourth damsel; then with but a minute's rest, the fifth. The hall rocked with applause. Then the sixth girl was serviced.

But when he got to the seventh, he could proceed no further. The audience felt bilked. The hall was filled with catcalls, and loud irate demands for refunds.

The producer was beside himself. He approached the performer. "Mon Dieu! You have ruined me!"

"I cannot understand it," the performer answered, "only an hour ago, in rehearsal, I was perfect!"

## Sangfroid

At a bar in Paris, an American was drinking with three Frenchmen. "Tell me," he asked, "what is *sangfroid*? Oh, I know that if you translate it, it means *cold blood*, but I'd like to know the connotation of that particular term."

"Well," answered one Frenchman, "let me try to explain. Suppose you have left your home—presumably on a business trip—and you come home unexpectedly. You find your wife in bed with your best friend. You do not get emotional; you do not get unduly upset. You smile at both of them, and you say, 'Pardon the intrusion.' Well, that is what I would call *sangfroid*."

Another of the Frenchmen standing by broke in and said, "Well, I wouldn't exactly call that *sangfroid*. I think *sangfroid* is just unusual tact. Suppose in the same situation you wave hello to your friend and your wife who are in bed, and with complete imperturbability you say, 'Pardon the intrusion, sir. Don't mind me. Please continue.' Well now, that's what I would call *sangfroid*."

"Ah!" broke in the third, "well, maybe, but as for me, I'd go a step further in my definition. If under the same circumstances you said, 'Pardon the intrusion. Please continue!' and your best friend in bed *could* continue—well, that's what I would call *sangfroid*."

## Laissez Faire

A man walked into a very expensive bakery shop where they made cakes to order.

"I'd like you to bake me a cake in the shape of the letter S," he said. "Can you do that?"

"Why certainly!" said the baker. "We can make a cake in any shape at all. When would you like it to be ready?"

"Have it ready by three o'clock tomorrow. I'll call for it," said the man.

The next day at three o'clock, the man came in for his cake. The baker proudly displayed the cake he had made. It was shaped like the letter S and decorated beautifully.

"Oh!" cried the man. "That's all wrong! That's not what I want. You made it in the shape of a regular printed S. I wanted a graceful *script* S. That won't do at all!"

"I'm terribly sorry you're so disappointed," said the baker. "We aim to please. I'll make you another cake at no extra charge. Don't worry."

"All right then," said the man. "I'll be back at six o'clock for the cake. And this time I hope it's right."

At six o'clock the man came in. The baker brought in the new cake. He was all smiles. "Isn't this a beauty!" he exclaimed.

The man looked at the cake. His face lit up.

"That's perfect!" he said. "Just what I wanted."

"I'm delighted," said the baker. "Now tell me, Sir, what kind of a box shall I put it in?"

"Oh, don't bother wrapping it up," said the man. "I'll eat it here."

**A** lady visited the zoo with her young daughter. She brought the little girl before the enclosure which held the elephants. The little girl turned to her mother and said, "Mother, what is that big thing the elephant has sticking out from his face?"

The mother answered, "Oh, that's the elephant's trunk. He picks up things with it, and he smells with it."

The little girl continued, "And mother, what is that long thing between the elephant's legs?"

"Oh," answered the mother, "that's the elephant's tail."

"No, no," said the little girl, "there's something else. There's something else that's sticking out between the elephant's legs."

The embarrassed mother answered, "Oh, that's nothing! That's nothing at all!"

A Frenchman standing by overheard the answer. Turning toward the mother, he blandly remarked, "Ah, I see! Madam is blasé!"

## Love Is Blind

A young Frenchman and a girl he was crazy about were driving down the Champs Elysées. He was fondling her; and she, in a paroxysm of frenzy, had unbuttoned his fly and was rubbing his dick.

He just couldn't stand the tension any longer, so he said to her, "Look, cherie, I can't wait till we get to the Bois de Boulogne. I must do it right away. Let's stop the car here, and we'll get out, and we'll get under it. We'll make believe we're fixing the engine." She agreed.

About 30 minutes later, the young man was tapped on the shoulder by a gendarme who stood over him.

"My dear young man," said the officer, "I do not disturb you because you have blocked traffic a full two miles down the boulevard. No, not for that. Nor do I disturb you because you have caused a crowd of 3,000 people to gather here at this spot. No, not for that. But as an officer of the law, it is my duty to inform you that your car has been stolen."

**T**he great François was entered in the annual three-mile swimming race down the Seine. An overwhelming favorite to win, he looked like a sure thing for the first ten minutes, as he splashed far ahead of his nearest competitor.

But then François spotted his girlfriend, Josephine. She was throwing kisses to him from the bank.

Suddenly, François fell behind. He seemed immobilized. His friend, Jacques, who had been following him along the shore, yelled frantically to him. "Francçis, why do you not move! You are losing the race! Move! Swim! Move!"

"Ah!" yelled back François, "It is that lovely creature Josephine! I took one look at her, and I got so excited, it is stuck in the mud!"

"Oh!" yelled back Jacques, "Then turn over and float!"

"Not so easy!" replied François, "I won't be able to pass the bridge ahead!"

Three Frenchmen were practicing their English. The conversation came around to a friend who was unhappy because his wife was childless.

"She is unbearable," said one Frenchman.

"No, that is the wrong word," the second replied. "She is inconceivable."

"No, no, you are both wrong," said the third. "What you mean is she is impregnable."

On the first day of her Riviera vacation, a beautifully proportioned young lady went up to the roof of her hotel to acquire a suntan as quickly as possible. Discovering there was not another soul on the roof, she slipped her bathing suit off and stretched out, face downward, with only a small towel stretched across her back.

Suddenly a flustered assistant manager of the hotel dashed onto the roof and gasped apologetically, "Miss, we don't mind if you sun on the roof, but we must ask you to keep your bathing suit on."

"What difference does it make?" the young lady demanded. "No one can see me up here, and I've covered my back with a towel."

"Of course," the assistant manager conceded, "but unfortunately you are lying on the dining room skylight."

"Hey, Jacques, I hear you won the lottery! That's wonderful!" exclaimed François, as he clapped his friend on the back.

'Thanks, Jacques," said François, "I guess sixty-three is just my lucky number."

Jacques was curious. "Well, tell me, how did you happen to pick out a number like sixty-three?"

"I had a dream," explained François. "I

dreamed I was in a theater, and on the stage was a chorus of sevens—each dancer a number seven, in a line exactly eight sevens long. So I chose sixty-three."

"But, François! Eight times seven is fifty-six, not sixty-three!"

"O.K., Jacques, so *you* be the mathematician!" said Francois.

## All a Matter of Mind

Coué, the renowned mind healer, was approached by a member of his audience. "My aunt is terribly sick, Monsieur Coué. I don't know what to do about it."

"Well," answered the master healer, "Your aunt only thinks she's sick. I repeat, she only *thinks* she's sick."

A week later, Coué gave another lecture, and the same woman came up to him. "Monsieur Coué . . ." she began. Coué interrupted and said "How's your aunt?"

"Oh!" answered the lady. "She *thinks* she's dead."

•

"Willie," the Sunday-school teacher asked a boy in the front row, "do you know where little boys and girls go when they do bad things?"

"Sure," Willie replied. "Back of the churchyard."

Voltaire was famous for his humanistic philosophy, but his penchant for satire also proved him an admirable wit.

Once he was told that a man he had praised was speaking poorly of him.

"Is that so?" Voltaire responded. "Well, perhaps we are both wrong."

"Jacques," said the amorous belle, "I hear my husband's footsteps on the stairs, and there's no other way for it, but you've got to jump out the window."

"What!" said the Don Juan. "How can I do that? We're on the 13th floor."

"Jacques," insisted the sweet one, "This is no time to be superstitious."

"Doctor, you must help me,' the pretty young lady told the psychiatrist. "Every time a boy takes me out, I always end up saying 'yes.' And afterwards I feel guilty and depressed."

"I see," the analyst nodded. "And you want me to strengthen your resistance?"

"Certainly not!" exclaimed the distraught girl. "I want you to weaken my conscience!"

# German Jokes

The head of one Berlin administration was approached by his secretary. "Herr Bahst," she said, "our files are becoming overcrowded."

"What do you suggest we do?" asked the busy administrator.

"I think we ought to destroy all correspondence more than six years old," answered the secretary.

"By all means," Herr Bahst responded, "go right ahead. But be sure to make copies."

## Ach Du Lieber!

The salesman walked into the hotel and noticed a pretty blonde lounging in a big easy chair.

He threw her a warm look which she returned with a smile and a nod. In a minute they walked over to the register arm in arm. The salesman signed, "Mr. and Mrs. Johann Schroder."

The next morning the salesman checked out. When he went to the cashier, he got a bill for $173. "What!" he shouted at the cashier, "I have only been here one night!"

"I know," said the cashier, "but your wife has been here for two months."

## Plain Talk

As death drew near, the rich young woman called her husband to her side and tearfully explained: "Arnold, I know that what I am about to tell you will come as a surprise, but I cannot die without this confession. I have been unfaithful to you with the chauffeur."

Her husband stared down coldly. "My dear," he said, "why do you suppose I gave you the poison?"

Frederick II of Prussia, also known as Frederick the Great, instituted social reforms and improvements throughout his country. One day, he unexpectedly visited a prison to inspect the facilities. The head jailer was dismayed to be asked to show the King through the jail itself to see the conditions personally.

As Frederick proceeded through the jail, the convicted men came running up to him, pleading innocence and begging for pardons. The King listened to all, and walked on. He became surrounded by men claiming they were not guilty.

One man, however, stayed in his corner. The King was surprised. "You, there," he called. "Why are you here?"

"Robbery, Your Majesty," stated the prisoner.

"And are you guilty?" asked Frederick.

"Entirely guilty, Your Majesty. I richly deserve my punishment."

The King parted the throng with his walking stick and pointed it at the jailer. "Warden," he said, "release this guilty wretch at once. I will not have him here in jail where by example he will corrupt all the splendid innocent people who occupy it."

While commuting home on the bus, Heilbroner glanced up from his magazine and found the man next to him dipping his hand into his hat and then waving his fingers in all directions. The hat, however, was completely empty.

Finally, curiosity got the best of Heilbroner and he asked, "Excuse me, sir, but why are you waving your fingers like that?"

The man smiled politely and replied, "I have a quantity of anti-tiger dust in my hat. I'm scattering it over the bus to keep the tigers away."

"That's ridiculous!" Heilbroner tittered. "There are no tigers within thousands of miles of here."

"Exactly!" the man grinned. "That's how powerful this stuff is!"

## No Doubt About It!

After hours of pacing in the hospital corridor, the nervous husband was informed by a nurse that he was the father of a baby boy. He tried to rush in to see his wife, but the nurse stopped him.

Again he paced the corridor. Then the nurse came out to announce a second baby. Once more the husband tried to force his way into the room, and once again he was halted.

Soon the nurse came out to announce another baby. This time, the husband pushed past the nurse and dashed into the delivery room. The doctor waved him back and yelled, "Stop—you're not sterile."

"You're telling *me*?" cried Herr Stoopnagel!

**O**skar turned to Friedrich and exclaimed in exasperation, "Ah, Friedrich, tell me, what can I do with that son of mine? The boy doesn't know how to drink, and he doesn't know how to play cards."

Friedrich was surprised. "What's the problem, Oskar? That doesn't sound bad to me. Why do you complain?"

"Because," replied Friedrich, "he drinks and he plays cards!"

## Oh! Those Laywers!

Herr Gumpert went to see his lawyer. He was quite distraught. "What am I going to do?" he asked. "Finkel is suing me for breaking an irreplaceable jar of his!"

The lawyer seemed calm. "Don't worry, Herr Gumpert," he soothed. "We have at least three lines of defense. In the first place, we will prove that you never borrowed the jar from Finkel. In the second place, we'll prove that when you borrowed the jar, it was already damaged beyond repair. And in the third place, we'll prove that when you returned it, it was in absolutely perfect condition."

Two well traveled Germans were sitting around discussing things when one of them asked, "What's the difference between heaven and hell?"

"Well," answered the other, "in heaven the British are the policemen, the French are the cooks, the Germans are the mechanics, the Italians are the lovers, and the Swiss are the hotel managers."

"And in hell?" pursued the other.

"In hell, on the other hand, the Germans are the police, the British are the cooks, the Italians are the mechanics, the Swiss are the lovers, and the French are the hotel managers."

In the midst of her psychiatric session, Mrs. Gottfried suddenly exclaimed: "I think I've taken a fancy to you, doctor! How about a kiss?"

"Absolutely not!" the doctor replied indignantly. "That would be contrary to the ethics of my profession. Now continue as before."

"Well, as I was saying," the patient continued, "I'm always having arguments with my husband about his father, and just yesterday—I'm sorry, but it just occurred to me again. What harm would there be if you gave me just one little kiss?"

"That's absolutely impossible!" the doctor snapped. In fact, I shouldn't even be lying on this couch with you!"

Two eminent psychiatrists, one 40 years old, the other over 70, occupied offices in the same building. At the end of a long day, they rode down in the elevator together. The younger man appeared completely done in, and he noted that his senior was still quite fresh.

"I don't understand," said the younger, "how you can listen to patients from morning to night and still look so spry."

The old psychiatrist shrugged his shoulders and replied, "Who listens?"

During World War II, a Nazi stowaway was caught on an American ship. A few minutes later, the transport was hit by a U-Boat.

The captain assembled everyone on board and gave them the bad news: "The ship is doomed. Can anyone pray?"

The Nazi stowaway said, "Yes, I can."

"Well," answered the captain, "you'd better get started. We're one life preserver short."

## Headstrong

Two women of old acquaintance ran into each other on a downtown street. "Why, Frau Donetz!" cried the first. "I haven't seen you in years! You look great, but whatever have you done to your hair? It looks exactly like a wig."

"To tell you the truth," said the second with some embarrassment, "it is a wig."

"Really? Well, you certainly can't tell!"

"Ah! Waldemar confided to his wife. "I've discovered a new position!"

"Is that so! " eagerly answered his wife. "What's that?"

"Back to back!" replied Waldemar.

"But that's impossible! We can't do anything back to back!"

"Yes, we can!" insisted Waldemar. "I've persuaded another couple to help out."

Mr. and Mrs. Gotbaum celebrated thirty years of marriage by going to a fancy restaurant. Awed by the elegant ambience, they nevertheless enjoyed selecting and tasting the strange-sounding dishes.

At the end of the meal, however, the waiter brought over two bowls of water and left them at the table. Mrs. Gotbaum looked at Mr. Gotbaum, and Mr. Gotbaum looked back at Mrs. Gotbaum. Neither of them knew what to do.

"Ask the waiter," suggested Mrs. Gotbaum.

"Are you kidding?" exclaimed her husband. "Show our ignorance? How embarrassing!"

"Yes," she said, "but it would be more embarrassing not to use them at all."

"True," said the man. So he called over the waiter and said, "Pardon me, but could you tell me the purpose of these dishes—of—of liquid?"

The waiter was polite. "Sir, those are finger bowls. You dip your fingers into the perfumed waters and then dry them on your napkin."

Mr. Gotbaum waited until the waiter left. Then he turned to his wife, and said, "See, Mathilda, you ask a foolish question, and you get a foolish answer!"

Steinberg had been having his lunch in the same restaurant for 20 years. Every day, he left his office at noon, went to the restaurant, and ordered a bowl of chicken soup. Never a change.

But one day Steinberg called the waiter back after receiving his soup.

"Yes, Mr. Steinberg?" inquired the waiter.

"Waiter, please taste this soup."

"What do you mean, taste the soup? For 20 years you've been eating the same chicken soup here, every day, yes? Has it ever been any different?"

Steinberg ignored the waiter's comments. "Please, taste this soup," he repeated.

"Mr. Steinberg, what's the *matter* with you? *I* know what the chicken soup tastes like!"

"Taste the soup!" Steinberg demanded.

"All right, all right, I'll taste. Where's the spoon?"

"Aha!" cried Steinberg.

"Doctor," complained the distraught mother, "I don't know what to do. My son insists on emptying ashtrays."

"Well," said the doctor, "that's not unusual."

"Yes, but in his *mouth*?"

## Horn of Plenty

Both partners in a clothing shop had been having an affair with Sally, the salesgirl, and both were shocked to learn that the young lady was pregnant. Each tried to lay the blame on the other.

Finally one of the partners went on a business trip, and while he was away young Sally was confined. Soon after, the partner on the road received a telegram from his associate: "Sally gave birth to twins. Mine died!"

A young doctor who was studying to be a psychoanalyst approached his professor and asked for a special appointment.

When they were alone in the professor's office, the young man revealed that he had a considerable amount of trouble with some of his patients. It seemed that in response to his questions, these patients offered replies which he couldn't quite understand.

"Well," said the older man, "suppose you ask me some of these questions."

"Why, certainly," agreed the young doctor. "The first one is, what is it that wears a skirt and from whose lips come pleasure?"

"Why," said the professor, "that's easy. A Scotsman blowing a bagpipe."

"Right," said the young doctor.

"Now the second question. What is it that has smooth curves and at unexpected moments becomes uncontrollable?"

The older doctor thought for a moment, and then said, "Aha! I don't think that's too difficult to answer. It's a major-league baseball pitcher."

"Right," said the young man.

"Now, Professor, would you mind telling me what you think about two arms slipped around your shoulders?"

"A football tackle," replied the professor.

"Right again," said the young doctor. "But you'd be surprised at the silly answers I keep getting."

## Fair Question

Essie and Gert went to visit their neighbor Rosie, who had just come home from the hospital with her triplets.

"Oh, Rosie, it's wonderful!" sighed Essie. "Imagine having triplets! I hear it's pretty rare."

Rosie replied smiling, "Rare? The doctor told me it's practically a miracle! He told me triplets happen only once in one million, six hundred and eighty times!"

"My God!" cried Gert. "Rosie, when did you ever have time to do your housework?"

## The World's Best Salesman

A man came into a grocery store and asked for five cents worth of salt. The proprietor asked, "What kind of salt do you want?"

"What kind of salt do I want? I want salt, plain and simple. How many kinds of salt are there!"

"Ha ha," chuckled the store owner, "what you don't know about salt! You come with me." And he took him downstairs and showed him a cellar that contained no less than 40 or 50 barrels of salt. The customer was amazed. "All these are different salts?" he asked.

"Yes, they're all different. We have salt for all kinds of prices and uses."

"My goodness, you're a specialist. I suppose, if you have all these barrels of different kinds of salt, you must sell one hell of a lot of salt. You must really know how to sell salt!"

"Oh," said the other, "me—I'm not so good at selling salt, but the guy who sold it all to me! Boy! Can *he* sell salt!"

**F**elix was a nice guy, but a social flop. Although he was 35, he had never conquered his childhood habit of bedwetting. Finally, one of his dear friends told him, "Look, Felix, you might as well know the truth. We're all very fond of you, but nobody can stand to come into your house because it smells, and you're driving your wife up a wall. Why don't you see a psychiatrist about your problem. Enuresis is not too uncommon and it can be cured Get it over with once and for all."

Felix was convinced. After six months of treatment he ran into the same friend. "Well, Felix, did you take my advice?"

"Yes," answered Felix, "I've been seeing a psychiatrist three times a week for about six months now."

"Well, have you had any results?"

"Oh," beamed Felix, "great results!"

"You don't wet your bed anymore?"

"I still do, but now I'm proud of it."

**A** man walked into a restaurant in a strange town. The waitress came over and asked him what he wanted.

Feeling lonely he replied, "Two fried eggs, and a kind word."

The waitress said nothing but went inside to give the order. When she came back with his food, the out-of-towner said, "Thanks for the eggs, but where's the kind word?"

The waitress leaned over and whispered, "Don't eat the eggs!"

Hummi and Gerti went to City Hall to apply for a wedding license. They were directed to the third floor where they had to fill out forms. When that was done, they were to take the forms to the sixth floor, pay a fee, and then they'd get their license.

They obediently filled out the forms, went up to the sixth floor and waited on a line. Eventually, they came to the front of the line, where the man looked over the forms.

"Gerti?" he said. "Your legal name isn't Gerti, is it? Go back to the third floor and fill out a new form with your real name, Gertrud."

So the couple went back downstairs, filled out another form, returned to the sixth floor, waited on line, and arrived before the man again.

This time the man got up to the part with Hummi's name on it. He frowned, "Hummi? That doesn't sound like a German name to me."

"Well, my real name is Humboldt," said Hummi, "but I've always been called Hummi---"

"Go back down to the third floor," interrupted the man, "and fill these forms out in German."

So the couple went down again, filled out another form, came back up to the sixth floor, waited again on line, and eventually arrived at the window. The names were okay this time, but the official found the address unacceptable. They had written 'Park, Bonn.' "*Park* is just a section of Bonn," said the man. "Go downstairs and rewrite the forms, and this time write 'Park Lea, Bonn' instead of 'Park, Bonn.'"

Hummi and Gerti went through the whole procedure yet another time and returned to the sixth floor. Finally, after several hours, everything seemed in order.

Hummi signed and turned to Gerti. "It's worth it, sweetheart. Now our little boy will know that everything is legal."

The official glared at them. "Did I hear you say you have a little boy?" Hummi admitted they did.

"You already have a baby and you're just getting a wedding license today? Do you know that makes your little boy a technical bastard?"

Hummi was icy. "So?" he countered. "That's what the man on the third floor said *you* are, and *you* seem to be doing all right!"

**A** man came to see a psychiatrist, and after an hour's conversation the doctor said, "You will have to come in twice a week for the next year. The fee will be $75 a visit."

"Okay," said the patient, "that takes care of you. Now how about me?"

## Irrefutable

A husband complained that his wife was a liar. "What makes you say that?" said his friend.

"Well," said the husband, "she came home this morning and told me she spent the night with Eleanor."

"Well," replied the friend, "Maybe she did. How do you know she's lying?"

"How do I know? Because *I* spent the night with Eleanor."

## The Good-For-Nothing

Two women met again after many years and began exchanging histories. "Whatever happened to your son?" asked one woman.

"Oh, what a tragedy!" moaned the other. "My son married a no-good who doesn't lift a finger around the house. She can't cook, she can't sew a button on a shirt, all she does is sleep. My poor boy brings her breakfast in bed, and all day long she stays there, loafing, reading, eating candy!"

"That's terrible," sympathized the first woman. "And what about your daughter?"

"Oh, she's got a good life. She married a man who's a living doll! He won't let her set foot in the kitchen. He gives her breakfast in bed, and makes her stay there all day, resting, reading, and eating chocolates."

## Hayseed

Two city men pulled up in front of a ramshackle country house and found a stubble-faced farmer on the front porch. "Hey, mister," the driver shouted, "can you change a twelve-mark bill?"

The farmer rose and nodded. "Sure thing, but I have to go inside to get the money."

The driver's companion said, "What a jackass! But what are you planning to do now?"

"I'm giving him a ten," the driver snickered. "I'll mark up the zero to look like a two. He'll never know the difference."

The farmer came out of the house with a battered wallet, took the bill the driver offered without examining it, and put it into his pocket. The he looked at the driver and said, "How do you want the change? Two sixes or three fours?"

**A** rotund woman in a crowded bus stepped on the foot of a gent who was trying to read his newspaper. "Madam," he snapped coldly, "kindly get off my foot."

"Then put your foot where it belongs," the woman snapped back.

"Don't tempt me, Madam, don't tempt me," he replied.

## Simple Arithmetic

Two professors were riding on a speeding train when they passed a large herd of sheep. "Quite a large herd, I'd say," the professor of biology said to his companion.

"Exactly six hundred twenty-five," replied the second, a professor of mathematics.

"Good heavens!" the first exclaimed. "Surely you can't have counted them all in that brief moment."

"Of course not!" the second shrugged. "I merely counted the legs and divided by four."

"I've got to get rid of Hans the chauffeur," complained the husband. "He's nearly killed me four times!"

"Oh!" pleaded his wife, "Give him another chance."

Hitler was having bad dreams, so he ordered his henchmen to find him someone to interpret them for him.

"Ah," intoned the seer, "I see that you are destined to die on a Jewish holiday."

Hitler frowned, but he was curious. "Which one?" he asked.

"It doesn't matter. Any day you die will be a Jewish holiday!"

# Hispanic Jokes

The Marriage Counselor was advising the bride-to-be. "The first thing I must tell you is that if you want to retain the interest of your husband you must never completely disrobe in front of him when retiring. Always keep a little mystery about you."

About two months later, the husband said to his bride, "Tell me, Marinda, is there any insanity in your family?"

"Of course not," she responded hotly. "Why do you ask such a question?"

"Well," said he, "I was merely wondering why, during the last two months since we're married, when you go to bed you never take off your hat."

In the midst of a heated argument, Mrs. Concha lost her patience and began beating her diminutive husband.

In terror he ran into the bedroom and crawled under the bed, his wife in hot pursuit.

"Come out!" she cried.

"No!" Mr. Concha shouted back from under the bed. "I'll show you who's boss in this house!"

## You Could Have Had It All!

José had worked as a tailor for many years. Came the time when he wished to retire, but his savings account was spare.

"Carolina," he confided to his wife, "I'm tired. I want to retire, but I don't know how we're going to afford it."

"Don't worry," said Carolina, "I have plenty of money." And she produced a bank-book with regular deposits stretching back over the entire forty years of their marriage.

"Where did this come from?" cried Jose in amazement.

"Well," said Carolina softly, "every time, during the last forty years, that we made love, I put five dollars away."

José threw his arms around his wife, and impulsively cried out, "Oh Carolina! For heaven's sake, you should have told me. If I had only known, I would have given you all my business."

Even a worm will turn, and the timid little husband confronted his wife and bellowed, "When are we eating?"

"Eight o'clock," she answered in a matter-of-fact way.

"Eight o'clock!" he roared, "I come home

at six o'clock from work! Tonight, we eat at seven o'clock, that's my deadline! And what's more," he continued, "don't give me any more canned salmon."

She turned, slightly astonished. The shy one, no longer shy, continued, "And set out my best suit—because I have got a date tonight with the blonde stenographer from the office. I'm sick and tired of this humdrum life, and I'm going out dancing."

The lady couldn't believe her ears. Carried away with his newly-found power, the husband continued, "And put out my little black tie! And when I'm all dressed and ready to go—" he said glaring at her full in the face, "do you know who's going to tie it on me?"

The big woman rose to her full height. "Yes," she said, "I certainly do! The man from the Miraflores Funeral Parlor."

Two Italians were sawing a large timber for a new subway. One of the men was big and thickset, the other was lean and diminutive. They used a large, heavy crosscut saw, each pulling back and forth.

A Pole happened to be passing by and he watched for a few minutes. Then he strode up to the big fellow, and said menacingly, "Give the saw to the little fellow if he wants it."

## Such Is Life

Jaime's wife was a constant nag, forever comparing her husband to his more affluent friends. "The Morellos have a new car and the Caballos just bought a new house," she complained. "All our friends live ten times better than we do. If we don't move into a more expensive apartment they'll all be laughing at us!"

One night her beleaguered husband Jaime came home and told her, "Well, we'll soon be living in a more expensive apartment. The landlord just doubled our rent."

## Who Can Argue?

An old woman living in New York died at the age of seventy-seven, leaving a grieving husband sixty-eight years old to survive her.

However, when a reporter came to interview the husband about their fifty years of marriage, the reporter surprised the bereaved in the living room with the maid on his lap, his arms entwined around her.

"I can't believe my eyes," squawked the reporter. "After fifty years of marriage, and your wife hardly buried!"

The widower dropped his arms abruptly and did some fast thinking. "In my grief," he said finally, "do I know what I'm doing?"

## Have a Heart!

The young husband and his bride flew to Miami for their honeymoon, and for days neither hide nor hair was seen of them. On the morning of the sixth day, they entered the dining room for breakfast. As the waiter approached them for their order, the bride turned to her husband and said coyly, "You know what I'd like, honey, don't you?"

"Yes, I know," he replied wearily. "But we've got to eat some time."

The honeymoon was barely over when the young couple got into their first argument. The subject was money.

"Before we were married," the wife cried "you told me you were well off."

"I was," he growled. "But I didn't know it."

## Smart Cookie

"Tell me the truth," the sick man told his doctor. "I want to know just how ill I am."

"Well," said the doctor, "you are very sick—very low. In fact, I feel that I should ask you if there is anyone you would like to see."

"Yes," murmured the patient feebly.

"Who is it?"

"Another doctor."

Carmen and Silvia got together for their usual morning cup of coffee.

"Did you meet that new woman who moved in across the street?" asked Carmen.

"Did I ever!" exclaimed Silvia. "She couldn't stop complaining about her husband."

"Believe me, there's nothing worse than a complaining wife," said Carmen. "Now take me; my husband drinks too much, he gambles, he stays out late—a worse husband you never saw in your life. But do *I* ever say anything to anybody?"

Mike Montez returned unexpectedly. His wife was nervous, and he became suspicious.

Then he saw a lighted cigar in the ashtray, and he yelled, "Where did this cigar come from?"

A voice from the closet answered, "Havana."

## Could Have Been Worse!

They met in the barber shop, and one of the men said, "Did you hear about that row last night on 128th Street?"

"No," said the other, "what happened?"

"Well, Luis Colón came home and he

found his wife in the arms of her lover. This guy went beserk. He had a blow torch in his pocket, and played it on the guy's legs. Then he took out his pliers and ripped out two of the guy's teeth. Then he stomped on him until the guy was half dead. And then he put carpet tacks on the stairs, and threw him down the whole flight."

"Well," replied the second man, "that sounds vicious and terrible, but it could have been worse."

"Could have been worse?" responded the first man, "what do you mean, it could have been worse?"

"Well, it could have been—because I was making love to that same babe the night before."

## Grave Peril

A man and his wife had a terrible argument, and the husband lost control and tried to throw her out of the six-story window.

The judge glared at the culprit and said, "What kind of a world are we living in? You have an argument with your wife, and you start to throw her out a six-story window. Do you know how dangerous that could be? She might land on somebody walking on the street."

## Repeat Performance

Two middle-aged men were seated at a bar talking when in came Raquel Jaspers, the gorgeous actress.

"Do you see her," said one, "that's Raquel Jaspers. She's one of the most beautiful women on the stage. You know, I feel like taking her out again."

"Taking her out again?" asked the other "When did you take her out?"

'Oh, I never took her out, but once before I felt like it."

"Mrs. Corneta," the gynecologist told the woman he had just examined, "I have good news for you."

"I'm glad to hear that," the young lady replied, "but I'm *Miss* Corneta."

"Miss Corneta," the doctor went right on, "I have bad news for you."

In Bolivia, a war correspondent saw a native riding on a donkey. Thirty feet behind him there trod a burdened woman who was struggling along under the blazing sun. The reporter was angered, and exclaimed "You no-good, why do you ride and let the lady walk?"

The Bolivian replied, "Well, she is my wife." Is that so?" responded the correspondent, "you heartless so-and-so."

"Well," said the Bolivian, "that is the custom down here."

Three years later, the correspondent again appeared on the scene. A new war was on. He ran across the same husband riding on a donkey with his wife carrying a heavy load. But this time she was walking in front of him. The reporter was outraged and said to the husband, "Still the same. You riding and she walking. Why is she walking in front of you—not behind you?"

Answered the husband, "Land mines."

**A** man went down to the Bowery and dropped into one of the cheap food joints. All of a sudden he seemed to recognize one of the waiters as an old pal of his.

"Say, Joe," he said, "I recognize you. You used to live down on First Avenue in my old neighborhood."

The waiter said, "Yes, I know you, too, Carlos."

"What the hell are you doing as a waiter in a terrible joint like this?" asked Carlos.

"Well," answered the other, "I don't eat here. What's your excuse?"

Carlos and his wife had an enormous family—fourteen children. Carlos could hardly make ends meet.

One day, he came to his wife and said, "Look. If you have another child, I'll just kill myself."

About a year later, his wife, Maria, broke the news. She was pregnant and was going to have another child.

Carlos didn't hesitate. He went over to his drawer, snatched his revolver, and put it to his temple.

But before pulling the trigger, he said, "Now, wait a minute. Maybe I am killing an innocent man."

"My son is going to win the marathon," exulted Mrs. Garcia.

"Oho!" sniffed Mrs. Ramon, "What makes you so sure?"

"Well," answered Mrs. Garcia, "the doctor says my son has the best example of athlete's foot he has ever seen."

The lad was boasting about the political situation in Nicaragua: "My uncle is a poor man, just a farmer, and he ran for alderman, and he made it. Six months later he ran for judge, and he made it. A year later, he ran for district attorney, and he made it. Two years later, he ran for governor of his province, and he made it. Then he ran for president of the republic, and he made it.

And then he ran for the border, and he didn't make it."

His wife was dying, and Ramon became very emotional. "Oh, my dear Lina, please don't die. I know it took a year for me to get you the mink coat you wanted, but if you only live, I'll buy you ten mink coats. You asked for a diamond ring, and it took me two years to buy one. But if you only pull through, I'll buy you ten rings."

Lina lifted up her head and tried to smile. "I'll try not to die, Ramon, but if I *should* die, make me one promise—bury me retail."

For nine rounds, the fighter had been taking a terrible beating. Through swollen lips he asked, "How am I doing?"

His second said, "As it stands now, you have to knock that guy out to get a draw."

A South American dictator was building a luxurious retreat for himself and his wife just outside his capital city. A rigid guard was established around the project to prevent the theft of valuable materials.

Each day at noon, the same workman appeared at the exit gate with a wheelbarrow loaded with dirt. The suspicious guard searched the dirt carefully each day, and even had it analyzed by a chemist to make sure nothing was being concealed. But the guard could find nothing to substantiate his suspicion, and, day after day, he let the workman pass.

A few years later, the guard met the same workman in the capital. The laborer was evidently enjoying great prosperity, and the guard was curious. "Now that it's all over," pleaded the guard, "just what were you stealing every day on that construction project?"

The workman grinned and answered, "Wheelbarrows."

José was upset. "Tomas, I lost my wallet and it had three hundred dollars in it!" he lamented.

Tomas tried to help José think. "Did you look everywhere for it?" he asked. "What about your coat pockets?"

José said, "Sure I looked. I tried all my

coat pockets, all my vest pockets, my front pants pockets, and my left hip pocket—and it just isn't anywhere."

"Your left hip pocket? Why don't you try your right hip pocket?" asked Tomas.

"Well," replied Jose, "that's the last pocket I have."

"So?"

"So, if I look in that pocket and if I don't find the wallet there, I'll drop dead!"

Returning home at 5:00 a.m., the husband found his wife sitting in the parlor in the embrace of a stranger.

Rushing to the offensive, she screamed at him, "And where have you been fooling around until five o'clock in the morning?"

Whereupon the husband yelled back, "Who's this man making love to you?"

And the wife sternly retorted, "Now don't you try to change the subject."

In geography class, the teacher asked. "Tinto, where's the Mexican border?"

"I don't know," said Tinto. "All I know is he ran away with my mother."

Carlos Jiminez owed the finance company one thousand dollars. After months of delinquency, he wrote to the company as follows:

Dear Sir:

I am sorry that I haven't paid my bill in all these months, and I feel thoroughly ashamed of myself. But I can now pay my bill and hold my head up high. Enclosed find my check to you for the thousand dollars I owe you.

Yours truly,
Carlos Jiminez

P.S. This is the kind of a letter I would have written you if I had the money.

There is a story about this perfectionist who spent two months forging a check. He got it down perfect, but then it came back marked "Insufficient Funds."

Voice on the phone: Is this the Salvation Army?

Answer: Yes, it is.

Voice: Is it true you save young girls?

Answer: Yes, it is.

Voice: Well, please save me one for Saturday night."

**A** marriage broker had been working on José Gonzales for a long time. He finally got him to pay a visit to a prospective bride.

After a sneak look at the girl, Gonzales whispered to the broker, "Why is one eye on top of the other? Why is her ear down on her neck? And why has she only got one nostril?"

The broker haughtily replied "It's obvious you don't care for Picasso."

**J**osé asked Roberto: "Why did you name your boy John? Every Tom, Dick and Harry in town is named John."

**W**hy do Puerto Ricans wear pointed shoes?

To step on the cockroaches in the corners.

**T**he judge glared at the prisoner.

"Why did you beat your wife?" he asked.

"Sudden impulse," explained the prisoner, "Uncontrollable impulse."

"Okay," said the judge, "I've got a sudden impulse myself. I'm going to put you away for 30 days."

"Well, that's too bad," said the prisoner, "you'll certainly put a crimp in our honeymoon."

Carlos was already in his twenties and he had never had a date with a girl, so his older brother decided it was time to do something about it. He arranged a blind date for Carlos with a nice young girl who was just as innocent as Carlos. But Carlos was very nervous. His hands became clammy and his tongue felt stiff as marble.

"Help me, Miguel. I don't know how to talk to girls. How can I be a good conversationalist like you?" asked Carlos.

Miguel had some advice to offer. "Listen, Carlos," he said, "I have a formula that never fails. Talk about family, food, and philosophy. Any of those topics is guaranteed to get a girl talking. Try it! I'm sure it'll work."

So Carlos went to meet the girl. She was pretty and shy. Carlos wanted very much to make a good impression. He thought of his brother's advice. First, he'd talk family.

"Tell me," he began nervously, "do you have a brother?"

"No!" came the girl's swift reply.

"Oh." Carlos was stymied, so he moved to the topic of food. "Do you like noodles?"

"No!" she said again.

But Carlos wasn't at a loss. He remembered his brother's advice. He'd talk philosophy. "Say," he said, "if you had a brother, would he like noodles?"

# Indian Jokes

Big Chief Black Fox visited New York in full regalia. Big Chief couldn't write, so he signed the hotel register with an "X."

The clerk turned to Big Chief and said, "You know, I could fix you up. Would you like a gorgeous blonde to call on you, let's say, in half an hour?"

"Sure," replied Black Fox, "that would be lots of fun."

Then the Indian went back to the register and crossed out the "X" and drew a square instead.

The clerk was puzzled and asked him what he was doing. "Well," replied Black Fox, "when I go out with a strange woman, I never use my right name."

Princess Sunflower had been absent from her tepee for several months, and she returned pregnant. Entering the tent, she raised her hand and greeted her father: "How!"

The old chief responded, "Never mind how! Who?"

A politician was campaigning in the state of New Mexico. To get the Indian votes, he traveled from reservation to reservation. At one spot, he promised new schools and a new college for all the Indians.

When they heard this, the Indians stood up and yelled, "Oompah! Oompah!" Five minutes later he promised hospitals, fully-staffed clinics, and kindergartens. At this, all the women of the tribe stood up, waved their arms, and shouted, "Oompah! Oompah!"

The politician was much taken by the invigorating response. He told the chief of the tribe that he would like to see the local playing field. The chief said he would conduct him to the playing field where the Indians kept their horses.

Said the chief, "All our horses graze in that pasture. On your way, please be careful not to step in the oompah!"

An Indian chief checks in at a swank hotel in Oklahoma city. An oil magnate comes up to his room to talk business. That afternoon, the oil man is found dead in the Indian's bathroom.

Accused of murder, the chief points to the toilet bowl, and says, "He pee in well."

# Irish Jokes

Jack ran into his friend Freddy on the corner just after Freddy had left a nearby bar. "Listen, Jack," Freddy grinned, "I've got a swell racket for you to try. I just went into that bar and ordered a drink. When the bartender asked for the money I told him I already paid him, and the absent-minded jerk believed me."

Jack immediately walked into the same bar and ordered a martini. The bartender served him and said, "Just a few minutes ago a guy came in here and—"

"What are you yammering to me about?" Jack interrupted. "Just give me my change."

## Advertising Medium

Returning home early from a visit to a relative, Mrs. Williams found her husband in the arms of the nextdoor neighbor.

"John!" she screamed in outrage. "How could you!"

Her husband merely glanced back from the heated embrace and scowled, "Uh-oh, here comes Mrs. Blabbermouth! Now the whole neighborhood will know."

## First Things First

Carson placed a frantic phone call to his doctor and explained that his wife, who always slept with her mouth open, had a mouse caught in her throat.

"I'll be over in a few minutes," said the doctor. "In the meantime, try waving a piece of cheese in front of her mouth."

When the doctor reached the Carson house, he found Mr. Carson waving a five-pound haddock in front of his wife's face.

"What are you doing?" exclaimed the doctor. "I told you to wave a piece of cheese. Mice don't like haddock."

"I know," Mr. Carson gasped, "But I've got to get the cat out first."

## The Affluent

Mike Flannagan had died. All his life as a plasterer he had been saving up, hoping to amass enough money so that he could buy himself a Cadillac and ride around town in style. When Mike suddenly passed away, he had just about accumulated enough money to make his wish come true.

The news of Mike's death shattered his friends. They got together to decide what kind of a funeral they should give him. One of them spoke up and said, "All his life, Mike wanted a Cadillac. Why don't we bury him in one? He left enough money for that." The friends agreed.

Four gravediggers were engaged to excavate a huge pit. Before the funeral, a crane had been put in place, and now a Cadillac was being lowered into the grave. Mike Flannagan was all dressed up in white tie, coat and tails, and was propped in back of the wheel. As the car was lowered into the grave, one of the gravediggers looked up, and to his amazement gazed at the sumptuous car in all its finery and at its sole occupant all tucked out in his swell duds. He exclaimed, "Gee! That's what I call living!"

Pat Moran appeared before the Naturalization Court. "Have you read Lincoln's Gettysburg Address?" queried His Honor.

"I have not, Your Honor."

"Have you read the Constitution of the United States?"

"No, I have not, Your Honor."

The judge then looked down at him and asked, "Well, Mr. Moran, what have you read?"

"Well, Your Honor, I have red hair."

## Tight Spot

Mrs. McCarthy moved to a new apartment in which there were new plumbing facilities. Elated at the sight of the bathroom, she plumped herself down hard on the seat only to find, ten minutes later, that she couldn't extricate herself.

In panic, she called Mr. McCarthy who tried to pull her out, but couldn't budge her.

"Well," said McCarthy, "there's nothing for it, but I'll have to call the plumber."

And for modesty's sake, he took his top hat out of the closet, and placed it over Mrs. McCarthy's pubic region. "It would be a slander and a shame," he murmured, "to let the plumber come and see Mrs. McCarthy in a state of sheer nakedness."

In a short time, Scanlon, the plumber, made an appearance. He took hold of Mrs. McCarthy's hand, and pulled and pulled, but he couldn't wrench her out of the seat.

He then turned to McCarthy and said, "Mr. McCarthy, I can chisel the seat away and save *her*, but the man's a goner!"

## A Bird in the Hand Is Worth. . .

Pat and Mike were walking down the street. Said Pat, "Mike, I've got awful cramps. If I don't take a shit right this minute, I'll pass out!"

"Okay," said Mike, "I'll stand a bit down the street and lay chickie. If anyone comes, I'll let you know."

Pat squatted and relieved himself. Then out of nowhere, Clancy the cop came parading down the street. Mike yelled, "Pat, here comes Clancy, and he's coming right toward us."

"Uh," cried Pat, pulling up his pants, "we'll have to do something quick." In a flash, he took off his hat and dropped it over the evidence

Up came Clancy, and eyed the two suspiciously. "And what have you got there under that hat?" the cop asked.

"Oh," said Mike, "we just caught a bird."

"Ah-hah," said Clancy, "a bird, is it? And you've got it under the hat?"

"Yes," said Pat, "That's where it is."

"Okay," offered Clancy helpfully, "you lift the hat very slowly, and I'll make a grab for it."

The athletic young man was practicing push-ups in the park. A drunk passed by and stopped to watch for a minute, "Shay, Bud," he slurred, "what happened to your girl?"

## The Vow

Tom O'Connor, Pat McCarthy, and Dennis Corcoran had been friends for many, many years. Every night they drank at the same corner saloon.

Then Dennis was taken sick. He brought his two pals together, confided that he wouldn't last very long, and said to them, "I want you to promise that every year, for the sake of old times, you'll each visit my grave and bring me a bottle of Scotch and lay it on the side in memory of the wonderful days we spent together."

The two men promised.

One year after Dennis had been laid to rest, on the anniversary of his funeral, the two men met at his grave. Pat took out a bottle of Scotch and lovingly placed it near the headstone. To his utter amazement, Tom unzipped his fly, took out his pecker, and pissed on the grave.

"Oh," cried Pat, taken aback, "is that the way you keep your promise to our poor departed Dennis?"

"I'm keeping my promise all right," answered the other. "I did bring him a bottle of Scotch and I gave it to him, but I didn't think he'd mind if the contents passed through my kidneys just once before I presented it to him."

## Sage Counsel

Sullivan walked into a saloon and ordered a glass of beer. "Say," he called out to the bartender after he'd been served, "how many kegs of beer do you use up every day?"

"Five," answered the proprietor. "Why'd you ask?"

"If I can show you how you can use up twice as much beer, will you buy me a drink?"

"Sure thing," the bartender agreed. "So how can I use up twice as much beer each day?"

"Easy!" said Sullivan. "Fill up the glasses!"

A customer in the cafe called the waiter to his table and asked, "Is this tea or coffee? It tastes like cough medicine."

"Well, if it tastes like cough medicine, it must be tea," the waiter replied. "Our coffee tastes like turpentine."

Flannagan came home drunk again. His wife couldn't stand it. She screamed at him, "If you don't stop this damnable drinking, I'm going to kill myself."

The hapless husband retorted, "Promises, that's all I get. Promises."

An old lady went to her physician and complained of constipation. The doctor asked, "Do you do anything about it?"

"Of course I do, doctor. I sit on the toilet for three hours every day."

"No, no, I don't mean that, Mrs. Hanley. I mean do you take anything?"

"Of course, doctor. I take along my knitting."

## Rock Bottom

"How is business?" asked Mike, as he walked into his friend's dress shop.

"Terrible," complained Jim. "Business stinks. Yesterday I only sold one dress, and today it's even worse."

"And how could it be worse?" asked Mike.

"How could it be worse?" wailed Jim. "Today the customer returned the dress she bought yesterday."

Pat and Tim were out hunting. As Pat aimed at the bird, Tim shouted "Don't shoot, the gun ain't loaded."

"Can't help it, Pat, I must shoot now. The bird won't wait."

**S**heila joined the girls for mah jongg one day, sporting a huge diamond ring. All the ladies were envious. Finally, one of them asked where she'd gotten it.

"Well," said Sheila, "my mother-in-law gave me a thousand dollars in trust before she passed away. She said that when she dies, I should buy her a beautiful stone for her memory. So I did!"

**W**ife, admonishing her husband, asked, "What did you get drunk for in the first place?"

Husband answers, "I didn't get drunk in the first place. I got drunk in the last place."

## Union Rules

When the noontime whistle blew at the construction site, O'Toole limped out for lunch.

"Why the limp?" his foreman asked. "You got a sore foot?"

"There's a nail in my shoe," O'Toole moaned.

"Then why don't you take it out?"

"What?" O'Toole replied indignantly. "On my lunch hour?"

When Mrs. Smith died, she went to heaven. St. Peter came to greet her. "Come in," he said.

Mrs. Smith answered, "Look, sir, I don't want to be here alone. I want to find my husband. I can't enjoy heaven unless we're reunited."

"Fine!" said St. Peter. "What was his name?"

"Joe Smith," she replied.

"Oh my God!" exclaimed St. Peter, "There are millions of Smiths in heaven, and thousands of Joseph Smiths. It would take ten years to locate him. Can't you tell me more about him?"

"Yes," answered the lady. "He was a very honest man, and a very mild man. His last words were, 'Annie, if you're ever unfaithful to me, I shall turn in my grave.'"

St. Peter broke out in a smile. "Oh, I know who you mean. You mean *Twirling* Joe Smith."

Hanrahan had just come into New York on a visit from Cork. His buddy, Morgan, met him and escorted him around the city.

"What's the name of that building?" cried Hanrahan.

"That's the Radio City. It cost forty million dollars, and took three years to build."

Hanrahan sneered, "We have got a building in Cork that's twice as tall, and only cost one million dollars, and we built it in four months."

They continued walking, and Hanrahan pointed to another structure: "What's that?"

"Well, that's the Empire State Building,' answered Morgan. "It cost four million dollars, and took two years to build."

"Why," sneered Hanrahan, "In Dublin we've got a building that's three times as large, and it took only one year to build, and we put up the whole shebang for only two million dollars."

Morgan was boiling. When they got downtown to the Woolworth Building, Hanrahan asked, "What's the name of that building?"

"Oh," loftily answered Morgan, "I don't know. It wasn't here this morning."

**P**at lay on his hospital cot. He was all bandaged up. In came Mike to see him.

"I am not very proud to see you," said Mike. "You have a fight with a guy only half your size, and you let that little pipsqueak knock you all over the lot."

"Okay, okay," interrupted Pat. "Stop—I won't have you speaking ill of the dead."

There once was a peasant who had five daughters, and his wife was expecting another child any day.

"Are you hoping for a boy or a girl?" asked the man's priest.

"It doesn't matter either way," said the poor man. "I can't afford either one."

A week later, the peasant family added twin girls to its flock, and the priest came to offer congratulations.

"I see that the Lord has smiled on you again," said the Father.

"Smiled!" frowned the peasant. "He laughed right out loud!"

A woman went to confession and told the priest she was having an affair.

"This must be at least the tenth time you've told me this story," the priest sighed. "Are you still involved with that man?"

"Oh, no, Father," she replied, "I just like to talk about it."

The young mother had just been delivered of a child, and her relatives gathered eagerly in the waiting room. Finally, a nurse brought out the infant swathed in a cloth.

"What is it?" asked an inquisitive aunt, running her hand up under the cloth. "Ah, it's a boy."

"Boy nothing!" the nurse snapped. "Let go of my finger!"

It was in Boston. A man ran up to a passerby and asked, "What's the quickest way to get to the Deaconess Hospital?"

The answer came back immediately: "See that crowd waiting for a streetcar. Just run over to that bunch and yell 'To hell with the Pope.'"

The wife staggered home. Her husband looked at her in amazement. "My goodness, Tillie, what happened to you? You have always been the epitome of sobriety. I have never seen you drunk before. How did you get this way?"

"Two Scotsmen ruined me," she replied.

"Well, I'll handle them, he said. "Who are they?"

"Haig & Haig."

A man with heart trouble won half a million pounds in an Irish sweepstake. The agent, who knew of the man's good fortune, was afraid to tell the lucky one for fear he might suffer a heart attack.

Instead, the agent went to the man's doctor and advised that the physician break the news to the winner during his next examination. The doctor agreed.

When Mr. McCartney came around to see him, the doctor said "And by the way, I heard you won half a million pounds in the sweepstakes."

"Is that so, Doctor? Well, I'm so appreciative of your good services that I am going to give you half of my winnings."

Whereupon, the doctor dropped dead.

Two of the boys in the club had been quarreling for years. One day the leader of the club intervened and said, "Fellows, it's time these shenanigans cease. We can't have this kind of ruckus every time we meet. Let's go across the street and have a drink and make peace."

"Okay," said both. So they sauntered up to the bar.

Mike lifted his glass and said, "Pat, here's wishing for you what you're wishing for me."

"Oh," replied Pat, "So you're starting in again."

## Recommendation

Dennis McCarthy was fired after twelve years with the same firm. He asked for a letter of recommendation, and the boss said "Well, it won't look good if I say I fired you. Let's say that you left," so he dictated a letter as follows:

"To Whom It May Concern: Dennis McCarthy has worked for me for twelve years, and when he left, I was perfectly satisfied."

An Irishman comes into a Dublin bar with a dog, and he makes a loud announcement: "I'll bet anybody in this saloon one pound I can make this dog do anything I want to."

Someone at the bar comes over and says, "Okay, I'll take that bet. Make the dog stand on his head."

So the owner calls the dog and says "Stand on your head." And the dog does just that immediately.

A third man comes over and says, "I bet I can make your dog do anything I tell it to." The owner is almost insulted. "You can?"

"Yes, for five pounds."

They both put up the money. The bettor takes the dog, puts it on a hot stove, and calls out "Get off!"

Mary was about to be married.

"James," she said to her future husband, "I might as well tell you the truth myself so you won't be finding it out after we're married. Two years ago, our family was so desperately poor and we were in such straits that for two weeks I had to become a prostitute to support my folks."

James was horrified. "Mary," he said, "there is simply no excuse for that. No matter how bad things were, you should not have permitted that to happen, even temporarily. I must call the marriage off."

Mary burst into tears and pleaded, "James, dear, surely you won't turn me away just because I was a fallen woman for two weeks. That's all over now.

All of a sudden, a light burst on James's face. "Oh," he said, "now I understand. You said *prostitute.* In that case, we will get married. I thought you said *Protestant.*

"Pat, how would you like to be buried in a Protestant cemetery?"

"Faith,' Tim, I'd rather die first!"

# Israeli Jokes

Shapiro had had a very good year, so he decided to take a cruise to France for the first time in his life. He was determined to savor every part of the trip.

The first night on board, Shapiro was shown to his place for dinner and found himself sharing a table with a well-dressed Frenchman. When Shapiro arrived, the Frenchman rose, bowed, and declared, "*Bon appetit!*"

Shapiro replied, "Shapiro!"

This same ritual took place at every meal. On the last day of the trip, Shapiro happened to run into the purser, and took advantage of the encounter to tell him what a pleasant table companion Mr. Bon Appetit had been.

"Oh, Mr. Shapiro," said the purser, "*Bon appetit* is not his name; that's just French for 'I wish you a hearty appetite.'"

"Is that so?" said Shapiro. He couldn't wait to rectify the situation. That evening, at dinner before his companion could do a thing, Shapiro stood up, bowed ceremoniously, and declared, "*Bon appetit!*"

Whereupon the Frenchman rose and replied, "Shapiro!"

## Modesty

The great rabbi lay dying. Devoted students flocked to his home to offer thier respects.

The rabbi's wife permitted only very old friends and close colleagues to come to his bedside. The visitors murmured words of high praise for their respected leader.

"So pious!" mourned one man, as he testified to the rabbi's devotion to God.

"So learned," grieved another, speaking of the rabbi's knowledge of the Torah.

"So charitable," said a third, speaking of the rabbi's generosity toward every one he encountered.

The great rabbi listened quietly and impassively to all the words of praise. Then suddenly he raised himself to speak. Everyone leaned close to hear the wise man's final words.

"Piety! Learning! Charity! Fine!" muttered the rabbi. "And about my great modesty, you have nothing to say?"

In the old country, there was a rabbi who traveled from village to village. In each town he would hold services and then stay for several hours while the congregation offered him their simple fare and asked questions.

The rabbi's means of transportation was a horse cart, driven by a sturdy, kindly fellow who admired the rabbi greatly. On every visit, after services, while the rabbi was being surrounded by the congregants, the driver would sit by patiently in the synagogue and listen.

After many years, the driver felt bold enough to ask the rabbi to grant one request. Just once, he'd like to feel the thrill of adulation. Wouldn't the rabbi trade places with him just once.

The rabbi wanted to please his loyal driver and granted the request.

The next day, the pair visited a new town. The rabbi and the driver exchanged garments. The rabbi quietly sat in the corner of the synagogue while the crowd gathered around the driver to feed him handsomely, and ask him questions. The driver handled the services and the questions very well for he had listened to his beloved rabbi for many years and he was entirely familiar with the stock questions.

Suddenly, a student arose and posed a complicated philosophical problem. The townsfolk turned to the driver, expecting a profound reply. But the driver knew he was stumped.

He hesitated for just a moment, and then he scoffed, "Young man, I am amazed that you should ask such a simple question. Why, even my driver, who is not well-versed in the Talmud, can answer that. And just to show you, we'll ask him!"

A farmer was on his way to town when he found a wallet in the road. Looking through the wallet he found $90, a name and address, and a paper stating: "If found, please return this wallet. $10 reward."

The farmer quickly changed routes and brought the wallet back to its owner. But instead of being grateful, the owner said, "I see you have already removed the ten dollars due you for your reward."

The poor man swore that he had not; the owner insisted that $10 was missing. "There was a hundred dollars in that wallet!"

So they took their tale to the rabbi, who listened patiently to the farmer, and then to the owner of the wallet. "Who will you believe, rabbi," ended the rich man, "that ignorant farmer or me?"

"You, of course," answered the rabbi. The farmer was aghast.

But then the rabbi took the wallet and handed it over to the farmer. Now it was the owner's turn to be astonished. "What are you doing?" he sputtered.

"You said your wallet contained one hundred dollars. This man says the wallet he found contained only ninety. Therefore, this wallet can't be yours," said the rabbi with finality.

"But what about my lost money?" cried the indignant man.

Patiently, the rabbi explained, "We must wait until someone finds a wallet with one hundred dollars in it."

The poor tailor was beside himself. His wife was sick and perhaps dying. He called on the only doctor nearby.

"Please, save my wife, doctor! I'll pay anything!"

"But what if I can't cure her?" asked the doctor.

"I'll pay whether you cure her or kill her, if only you'll come right away!"

So the doctor promptly visited the woman, but within a week, she died. Soon a bill arrived charging the tailor a tremendous fee. The tailor couldn't hope to pay, so he asked the doctor to appear with him before the local rabbi to arbitrate the case.

"He agreed to pay me for treating his wife," stated the physician, "whether I cured her or killed her."

The rabbi was thoughtful. "Well, did you cure her?" he asked.

"No," admitted the doctor.

"And did you kill her?"

"I certainly did not!" expostulated the physician.

"In that case," the rabbi said with finality, "you have no grounds on which to base a fee."

## A Lady Must Eat

A butcher was going over his account books and found that Mrs. Levy owed him a sizable sum of money. He called her on the phone several times, but could never get in touch, so he decided to send her a letter.

"Dear Mrs. Levy," he wrote, "please pay up the money that you owe me."

The next week, he received a reply in the mail: "I can't pay right now, but please send me two good chickens, four pounds of hamburger, and six steaks."

The butcher was angry. He wrote again: "Dear Mrs. Levy: I will send your order when you pay up your account."

The reply came the next day: "I can't wait that long!"

## Fantastic!

It was a broiling day in July. Mrs. Finkelstein went into a store to buy a fan.

"What kind fan do you want?" asked Levy, the storekeeper. "We have fans for a nickel, for a quarter, and for a dollar."

"So give me one for a nickel," said Mrs. Finkelstein.

"O.K." said Levy, as he handed her a thin Japanese paper fan.

In ten minutes, Mrs. Finkelstein was back.

"Look what trash you sold me!" she shouted. "The fan broke."

"It did?" said Levy. "And how did you use it?"

"How did I use it?" replied Mrs. Finkelstein. "How do you use a fan? I held it in my hand, and I waved it back and forth in front of my face. Did you ever?"

"Oh no!" explained Levy, "With a five-cent fan, you got to hold it still, in both hands, like this, and wave your head back and forth in front of it."

**M**r. and Mrs. Mandelbaum decided the only solution to their marital problems was in divorce. So they went to see the rabbi.

The rabbi was concerned about the three children and was reluctant to see the family broken up. He thought that if he could stall the couple maybe they would work it out together.

"Well," said the rabbi, "there's no way of dividing three children. What you'll have to do is live together one more year. You'll have a fourth child, and then, it will be easy to arrange a proper divorce. You'll take two children, and he'll take two."

"Nothing doing," said Mrs. Mandelbaum. "Rabbi, if I depended on him, I wouldn't even have had these three!"

Joe left on an extended trip to Europe and left his cat in the care of his brother. Of course he gave him the itinerary, just in case of an emergency. Sure enough, after Joe was gone two weeks he gets a call from Sam. "What's the matter Sam? Is anything wrong?"

"Yeah, your cat died."

"My cat died? I can't believe it.' What a shock. I can't take it in. Sam, how could you do this to me? How could you spring such news on me without warning like this?

"Gee, I'm sorry, but what else could I do?"

"Well, at least you break it gradually, so I get used to the idea. You call and say "Listen, Sam, I think I have bad news. Your cat ran up on the roof and we can't get her down."' Then I'd tell you to call the police. You'd call back the next day and you'd say 'I called the police, but when they went to get your cat down, she had an accident and now she's in the hospital.' So I'd say, "OK Sam, just give her the best care money can buy.' Then you'd call back the next day and you'd say, 'Sam we did all we could, but your cat died.' By this time I'd be ready for the bad news."

"I see, Sam, and I'm truly sorry," said the contrite Joe.

A few days later, Sam gets another call.

"Hello, Sam, listen this is Joe. I have to tell you—Mom's on the roof."

Mildred met Sally in the park. "You look simply wonderful, Sally," said Mildred.

"Well, perhaps that's because I'm having an affair," said Sally slyly.

"Yeah, who's catering it?"

A man and his wife came to the village rabbi. The woman poured out a long history of her misery at the hands of her husband. "I can't stand it!" she wound up with. "He's awful!"

The old rabbi took her hand and said, "You're right."

Next it was the husband's turn. His story was just as accusing. He complained tearfully about his wife's behavior, citing many misdeeds.

The rabbi patted the man gently on the back, and said to him, "You're right."

A student who had been permitted to listen to both interviews now approached the rabbi, and whispered, "How can it be, rabbi? You told her *she* was right, and now you tell him *he* is right. How can both of them be right?"

"Ah!" answered the rabbi. "You're right, too!"

## Self-Reliance

In 1948, when Israel declared its independence, Velvil Pasternak flew at once from New York City to offer his services to the fledgling state. He applied at the recruiting office to join the beleaguered Israeli Army.

After the usual forms were completed, he was told to go down to Section 1 and pick up his Army gear. He came to the first window and the clerk asked him what size shoes he needed.

"Size 8-1/2," answered Velvil.

The clerk looked around in the stockroom, came back and said, "I'm sorry, we don't have 8-1/2. We're very short of shoes. We got size 8 and we got size 9, but no 8-1/2's."

Velvil hesitated, but the clerk advised, "Look, what do you need shoes for? You got sneakers on. It's perfectly okay. Better than to have shoes that are too small or too big. Forget about shoes. Wear your own sneakers."

Velvil agreed and went to the next window, where he requested a medium-size army shirt. The clerk looked around and came back. "Look, we got size small army shirt and size extra large. Medium we ain't got." Then he looked at Velvil and said, "Look, that shirt that you've got on. That's pretty good. What do you need an army shirt for? Use what you've got."

Velvil agreed and moved on. He went through this at each commissary window and came out with his original set of clothes.

He was then ushered into the medical office. The doctor examined him and asked a few standard questions. "Do you swim?" he asked.

"What!" exclaimed Velvil. "Ships you ain't got neither?"

The students attending an international university were asked to write papers dealing with the elephant in any way they chose.

A German student wrote a fifty-page paper, called *An Introduction to the Study of the Elephant.* He also had thirty extra pages of footnotes and bibliography.

A French student handed in a short, beautifully lettered work, entitled *The Elephant and His Love Life.*

A British student created an illustrated travel guide, and he titled it *Hunting the Elephant in Deepest Africa.*

An American student wrote a paper which he called *How to Raise Elephants in Your Backyard for Fun and Profit.*

And the Jewish student wrote a paper on *The Elephant and Anti-Semitism.*

## Foreign Intrigue

The Russian Intelligence Agency intercepted a message that showed that Israel had just made an important atomic discovery. Anxious to find out what the Israelis were up to, a Russian agent was dispatched immediately.

The mission was top secret. The agent chosen was a very trusted and experienced man. He was given a name to contact in Tel Aviv, a guy by the name of Weinstein. The password was "Volga boatman."

The agent flew to Tel Aviv one evening. Early the next day he went to look up the contact. To his dismay, when he arrived at the apartment house, he found that three different Weinsteins were listed as living there.

There was nothing to do but try them all one at a time, hopefully hitting the right one the first time. The agent knocked on the door at the first floor. "Yes?" said a man.

"Is your name Weinstein?" asked the agent.

"Why, yes," replied the Israeli.

"Volga boatman," said the Russian.

"Oh," grinned the man. "You want Weinstein the spy. He lives two flights up."

## Don't Count on It

Israel has always encouraged immigration. But

for a while it looked as if there wouldn't be enough money to care for newcomers as well as for the already established Israelis. The financial situation was bad.

Several cabinet members met to discuss the situation. "I have an idea!" said one. "Why don't we declare war on the United States? They're bound to win, and you know how they treat their victims. They'll come into our vanquished country and build up our industry, give us money for roads, food for relief, and so on!"

"That's a wonderful idea," replied another minister. "But what if, with our hard luck, we win?"

In synagogue on Yom Kippur, the solemn Day of Judgment, a rich Jew stood at his seat and prayed in a loud whisper, "Oh Lord, I am the lowest of the low. I am unworthy of your goodness. I am a nobody, a nothing!"

Immediately, in the row directly in back of him, a poor piece goods cutter raised his voice in prayer, "Oh Lord, my God, please forgive my sins for I am nothing!"

Whereupon, the first man turned around in disdain. "Look who claims he's a nothing!"

## Nudnick!

Mr. Feldstein had gone to synagogue faithfully twice a day ever since his bar mitzvah. Every morning he lay *tfillin.* He had consulted God every time he took a new apartment, every time he had to decide on a name for a child, every time he had a problem with his business.

Yet when he turned 65, he was still a poor man. What was worse, his brother-in-law had never even come near a synagogue, and yet he was a millionaire! Mr. Feldstein couldn't understand it. So once more he went to God.

"Oh, God, have I not come to you with every event in my life? Am I not your obedient servant? Yet you make Morris a millionaire and me you make a poor man? Oh God, why is this?"

A sigh came up from the altar. Slowly the voice of God came in heavy tones. "Because, Feldstein, you're such a nudnick! All you do is nag me!"

**M**r. and Mrs. Goldfink were worried. All their friends' children had expressed their wishes about what they were going to grow up to be—firemen, policemen, whatever. But their little five-year-old had said nothing about a future career.

"I'll tell you what we'll do," said Mr.

Goldfink. "We'll put him in a room, all alone, with only a Bible, an apple, and a silver dollar. If he reads the Bible, it means he's going to become a rabbi. If he eats the apple, he wants to be a farmer. And if he plays with the dollar, he's headed for banking."

So the parents put their boy into the room with the three items and waited half an hour. Then they went in to see what he was doing. He was sitting on the Bible, eating the apple, and had put the silver dollar in his pocket!

"What does that mean?" whispered Mrs. Goldfink to her husband.

"It means he's going to be a politician!"

## Earmarked

A delighted grandmother was asked to babysit for an afternoon with her daughter's two little boys. The happy trio set off for the park and a picnic.

On the way, the woman ran into an old friend. "How are you?" she greeted her warmly.

"I'm very well, thank God," replied her friend. "And these must be your grandchildren. How old are they?"

The grandmother puffed up with pride. "Oh! The lawyer," she said pointing, "is two, and the doctor is going on four!"

**A** rabbi asked a rich Jew for a contribution for the poor. The man refused.

"Why should I give them what I worked so hard to earn?" he demurred. "They're poor because they didn't work as hard as I did."

The rabbi said nothing for a moment, then bade the wealthy man to go to the window. "Look outside and tell me what you see."

"I see—people," the rich man said.

"Now look in this mirror," commanded the rabbi. "What do you see now?"

"Myself."

"Yes, quite astonishing," continued the rabbi, "when you cover a piece of glass with some silver, all you can see is yourself."

## Just One Little Fault

A matchmaker told a young man that he had the perfect girl for him. "She's a redhead!" he exclaimed with pride.

"You mean Becky, the tailor's daughter?" cried the young man.

"That's her!" beamed the matchmaker.

"You're crazy! She's almost blind!"

"That bothers you? That's a blessing; half the time she won't be seeing what you're doing."

# Italian Jokes

**T**wo peddlers were standing in the street talking. They had plenty of time to talk because they had very little business.

One said, "You know, if I had Rockefeller's money, I'd be even richer than Rockefeller."

"What!" cried the other, "How could that be?"

"Because," explained the first, "I'd have all of Rockefeller's money besides what I make from the pushcart."

## You're So Hard-Hearted!

When Luigi's wife died, the young widower was wild with grief. At the funeral he sobbed uncontrollably; at the cemetery he almost fainted.

"Ey, Luigi," a friend soothed him in the limousine driving back, "I know it's rough now, but in six months you'll find another beautiful girl and get married again."

Luigi turned on him and glowered. "Six months! What am I gonna do *tonight*?"

## Stand To Treason

Pasquale was being examined for naturalization as a U.S. citizen. "Who is the president of the United States?"

The foreigner answered correctly.

"And the vice president?"

Again he gave the right answer.

"Could you be president?"

"No! No!"

"Why not?"

"I'm too busy. I work in the barber shop all day now."

Giovanni Balbo was upset. His father, a good man, was having trouble sleeping, and there was nothing the son could do to help. He gave the man ear plugs, pills, warm milk and honey, but nothing worked.

One day, Giovanni heard about a very expensive hypnotist who claimed he could suggest anything to a person's subconscious. He was especially noted for his work with insomniacs. So Giovanni called on the man, agreed to pay his huge fee, and made an appointment for him to come to the house.

The hypnotist came, and told Mr. Balbo to lie down on the couch. Slowly, he twirled his shiny watch before the man's eyes and spoke gently, softly, soothingly, watching the eyes begin to droop. "Relax, Mr. Balbo," he cooed. "Look at the gold watch—watch it move—you are getting sleepy—you are feeling heavy—so sleepy—you can't keep your eyes open—"

Mr. Balbo's eyes were closed now, and he was breathing smoothly and deeply. Giovanni, who was almost alseep himself, tiptoed out of the room with the hypnotist. He wrote him a large check, and showed him to the door with effusive thanks.

Then quietly he went back in to where his father lay peacefully. In the semidark room, Giovanni looked fondly on his father's relaxed face. Then suddenly, the man's eyes flew open and the voice was strong. "Well, Giovanni, has that crazy guy left already?"

**W**hat do they call removing a splinter from an Italian's behind?

Brain surgery.

**S**ign In Wine Factory: Any Italian who wishes to attend the funeral of a relative must tell the foreman of his department on the day before the game.

## Such Fine Business

Pasquale was fed up with his gas-eating station wagon, and sold it to his friend Tony for $500. But the next day, Pasquale began to miss the old crate, and offered to buy it back from Tony for $550. So Tony sold him the car. The following day, he looked up Pasquale.

"I'm sorry I sold the car back to you, Pasquale," he said. "I'll give you $600 for it right now."

So Tony bought the car back. The next day Pasquale again regretted the sale, and bought it back for $650.

The next day, Tony came to buy the car back, but learned Pasquale had sold it to his cousin.

"You idiot! Why did you sell it to an outsider?" chided Tony, "especially when we were both making such a great living out of it!"

**W**hat do they call an Italian submarine captain?

Chicken of the sea.

**H**ow do you break an Italian's finger?

Punch him in the nose.

**W**hy does time go by so fast in Italy?

Because every time you look around you see another Dago by.

Kidnappers grabbed an Italian lad and two days later sent him home with the ransom note.

Then the parents sent the kid back with the money.

What happens when an Italian housewife doesn't pay her garbage bill?

They don't bring her any more.

Why did Mussolini have five bullets in him when he was found dead?

Because 200 Italian sharpshooters were firing at him.

A philanthropist had donated a swimming pool to the Society of Italian Brothers. When he came over to visit, he asked the caretaker, "Well, how do they like it?"

"They're crazy about it," came back the answer. "We can't keep them out. And I'll bet they'll like it even better when we put water in it."

Have you heard about the Italian showgirl who said she'd do anything for a mink coat and now she can't button it?

A matchmaker proposed a beautiful young girl to a businessman client as a possible bride. The client was reluctant to pursue the matter because he didn't possess, in his opinion, enough money for such an attractive girl.

"Oh, you needn't worry about that," assured the matchmaker. "You'll never have to support any of her family; the girl is an orphan."

The meeting was arranged. Several weeks later, the man complained to the matchmaker. "You lied to me!" he said. "The girl is not an orphan. She not only has a father who's alive and well, but he is living in prison!"

The matchmaker shrugged. "You call that living?" she asked.

Did you hear about the Italian who broke his arm raking leaves?

He fell out of a tree.

What is the best way to grease a Ferrari?

Run over an Italian.

Tony: Every night I dream of a sign on the door and I push and push but I can't open it.

Patsy: What does the sign say?

Tony: Pull!

When Scamarella, the garment cutter, got back from his vacation in Italy, he eagerly told his friends in the garment district all about it.

"I even was in a group that went to the Vatican," he said proudly. "And I got in to see the Pope!"

"The Pope!" One man was awed. "What did he look like?"

"Oh, he's a nice man. Thin and spiritual-looking. I figure a size 43, short."

Did you hear about the Italian hold-up man?

He sells brassieres.

A matchmaker took a well-to-do man to meet a prospective bride and her family. While they were waiting in the living room, the matchmaker pointed to the elegance of the surroundings.

"These people are well off. Look at this fine furniture. Take a look at the delicate dishware. Notice the paintings on the wall and the sculpture on the mantel."

The businessman was suspicious. "To make a good impression on me, perhaps they have borrowed these things."

At that, the matchmaker scoffed, "Borrowed? Don't be foolish! Who would lend anything to such paupers?"

Do you know why Polish jokes are so short?

So Italians can understand them.

Why don't they give Italian elevator operators a ten-minute break?

Because they would have to retrain them.

Have you heard about the Italian who makes his own sparkling burgundy?

He uses two bottles of red wine and a bicycle pump.

Why did the Italian lose his job as an elevator operator?

He couldn't learn the route.

Two old friends from Sicily emigrated to New York. One day they met on the street, and Pasquale said, "This is a wonderful country. Where in the world could you ever walk down the street, meet a complete stranger who takes you to dinner, and then invites you to spend the night at his house?"

Giuseppe: "Did this happen to you?"

"No," said Pasquale, "but it happened to my sister."

## Heredity

The world's greatest male pickpocket met the world's greatest female pickpocket, and they got married. In time, she went to the hospital to have a child.

The doctor had an awful time during the delivery, and the baby was born with one fist clenched tight. The doctor tried everything to pry open the hand. It took him the better part of twenty minutes to succeed. When he finally pried the little fist open, what do you think was in the child's hand—the doctor's wrist watch.

"Oh, boy!" he cried ecstatically, "I'm so happy. I'm going to marry an American girl."

"No, no Pasquale," his mother pleaded. "American girls aren't much good. An American girl can't cook, she doesn't know how to make love, she always fights, and what's more, she's going to wind up calling you a wop."

But Pasquale didn't listen. He married the girl, and thirty days after the honeymoon he called up his mother.

"Mama, Mama, you're wrong," Pasquale shouted happily. "Emelina is a good cook, she's wonderful in bed, and Mama, the only time she calls me *wop* is when I call her *coon.*"

**A** man consulted a psychiatrist for help with various problems. The analyst said, "Stretch out here on the couch. Just relax and tell me about your early life. Just keep on talking. Say anything that comes to mind."

The man proceeded to spill out his life's story. Suddenly the analyst took out a big balloon and, sitting behind the patient, blew it up to full size. Then he stuck a pin in it. The balloon burst with a loud crash. The patient was startled. The doctor said sharply, "Now tell me, quick, what did you think about when you heard the loud explosion?"

"I thought of sex."

"Sex? At such a moment? You thought about sex?"

"Well," said the patient, "what's so surprising about that? It's all I ever think about."

## Unassailable

Luigi, just out of school, got a job in a bank. The first day he was there, the cashier tossed him a package of bills.

"Here," said the cashier, "count these and see if there are 100."

Luigi, started counting. He got up to 60, stopped counting, and threw the package into a drawer, saying to the man next to him, "If it's right this far, it's probably right all the way."

What's the easiest way to sink the Italian Navy?

Put it in the water.

A man has been asked by his wife to bring home a canary. He goes into a pet shot and picks out a good looking bird.

As the shop owner is about to wrap up the cage, the man says, "Wait a minute. I see that bird has only one leg."

"So what?" answers the shop owner. "What are you looking for—a singer or a dancer?"

A woman reputed to have been born in Milan challenged a number of beachgoers to a race, and proceeded to outswim the four strongest natators on the beach. Everyone was wondering where she could have learned to swim so well.

"Oh!" she explained, "For three years I was a streetwalker in Venice!"

A plane was flying over the Bay of Naples. The pilot turned to a passenger and said, "Have you ever heard the expression, 'See Naples and die?"

"Yes I have," said the passenger.

"Then take a good look." said the pilot, 'Our propeller just fell off."

Alfredo and Pauli sat down at noon to eat their lunch. Pauli opened his lunch box and said, "Oh my God! Peanut butter sandwiches again. I hate peanut butter." He bit into one and made a terrible face.

Alfredo watched him do this every day for a week, then turned to him and said, "Pauli, if you hate peanut butter that much, why don't you tell your wife not to make you peanut butter sandwiches?"

"What wife," screamed Pauli, "Whose wife? I don't have a wife. I make my own sandwiches."

## Shoemaker, Stick To Your Last

At an examination for citizenship, an Italian was asked by the judge, "How many states are there in the Union?"

"I don't know," replied the applicant. "If I asked you how many bananas there are in a bunch, you wouldn't know. You know your business, and I know mine."

Italian guide: We are now passing the most fabulous brothel in Rome.

Male tourist: Why?

A man walked into a barber shop and said "A hair cut and a shave—and silence, please." Giuseppe, the barber paid no attention, and started his monologue. Giuseppe talked, and talked, and talked.

The customer got out of the chair, went over to the boss and said, "Would you stop this barber from talking."

"I can't stop him. According to the Constitution of the United States, he is a free citizen and he has a right to talk."

"I know it," shot back the customer, "but the United States has a constitution that can stand it. My constitution can't."

The hood's son was on a quiz program. The gangster attended the show. The kid was asked, "Now for fifty thousand dollars, tell me who shot Abraham Lincoln."

The kid was baffled. He just sat, stared, and squirmed, but not a word came out of him.

"Ah!" gloated the crook, "That's my boy! He ain't no stool pigeon."

What do you call an Italian who marries a Negro?

A social climber.

## Isn't It So!

Sal tried to get a job with the railroad. They gave him a test.

"Now," said the examiner, "suppose two trains were headed for each other at eighty miles per hour on the same track. What would you do?"

"I'd grab a red flag," said Sal, "and wave to them to stop."

"But suppose you can't find a red flag?" pointed out the examiner.

"Then I would take a switching iron and change the tracks."

"And suppose you can't lay hold of a switching iron?"

"Well, in that case," offered Sal, "I would call up my wife, Maria."

"What's your wife got to do with two trains heading toward each other at eighty miles an hour?" queried the personnel director.

"Well," said Sal, "I would tell her to come down because she would be about to see the biggest smashup in history."

An old Sicilian was going to the mountains for the first time in his life. He was poor, so he had to go by bus, but that didn't dent his spirit. He was so happy that he began singing as soon as he boarded the crowded vehicle.

The driver had been going for many hours, and wasn't too pleased about having the old man standing in the aisle right behind him, singing at the top of his lungs. And he told him so.

But the singing didn't stop; and after several vain exhortations, the driver warned the man that if he didn't cut out the singing, he'd stop the bus and toss out his valise. Even this threat didn't quiet the old man. Fifteen minutes later, the driver pulled off the road, walked up to the old man, picked up the valise, and threw it out the nearest window.

Then the driver returned to his seat. But the singing continued. Finally the driver listened to the words: "I'm going to the mountains! I'm going to the mountains! I won't call the police! I didn't bring a valise!"

A hoodlum wanted to join the mob. In order to qualify, he had to cite his record. The applicant began as follows: "Last April I robbed the 1st National Bank. In May, I robbed the 3rd National Bank."

The leader of the mob interrupted, "And what was the matter with the 2nd National Bank?"

"Well, that's where I keep my money," the hood replied.

A man visiting a Roman bordello was warmly greeted by the proprietress. After an exchange of pleasantries, the client said, "And by the way, how is your husband Tomasso?"

"Oh," she answered sadly. "He died about six months ago."

"I'm sorry to hear that," said the client. "He was one of the greatest pimps I ever met."

"Thank you," answered the madam. "Isn't that just like life. A man has to die before somebody says anything nice about him."

An Italian, an American, and a Russian had an argument. The Russian declared, "We will be the first to land on Mars."

The American said, "We have landed on the moon more than ten times. We will be the first to land on Mars."

Then the Italian broke in, "You can fight all you want about who'll be the first to land on Mars, but we Italians will be the first to land on the sun."

"You're crazy," said the American. "You can't land on the sun. It's too hot."

"You think we're stupid or something," said the Italian. "We know that. We're going to land at night."

# Jewish Jokes

## Perspectives

The week after Labor Day, Abe Cohen and Nat Goldfarb met for lunch. They hadn't seen each other for several months. As they sat down, Abe began complaining.

"Nat, my friend, I have just lived through a summer the likes of which I never thought I would see. June was already a disaster. Never in my entire business career have I seen a June like that. Yet when July came I realized that June had been quite good, for with July I went down through the floor and into the sub-basement. July was absolutely unbelievable and indescribable, and when I tell you—"

But at this point Nat interrupted impatiently. "For heaven's sake, Abie, why are you coming to me with these piddling matters?" he said, even more depressed than his friend. "If you want a tale of *real* trouble, here it is. Yesterday my son, my only son, on whom I had been placing all my hopes, came to me and told me he was getting married to another boy. Do you hear me? My son has become an open homosexual! What can be worse than *that*?"

"I'll tell you," Nat answered, "August!"

Poor Mrs. Eisenberg was beside herself. Her husband had left her, and her daughter Sally was thirty-two years old and still unmarried. She thought about it and worried about it and finally decided to take some action.

"Sally," she said, "I think you ought to put an advertisement in the paper." Sally was aghast at the thought.

"No, listen," said Mrs. Eisenberg, "it sounds wild, but I think we should try it. You don't put your name in, just a box number. Here, I wrote one up already." And she showed Sally an ad she had devised:

*Charming Jewish Girl, Well-Educated, Fine Cook, Would like to Meet Kind, Intelligent, Educated, Jewish Gentleman. Object: Matrimony.*

Sally was embarrassed, but she couldn't talk her mother out of it. So into the paper the ad went. And Sally went every day to see if there were any replies.

A few days later, there was a letter for her. Sally ran home to her mother flushed with excitement. "Look!" she cried.

"Well, hurry up and open it!" urged Mrs. Eisenberg. So Sally tore open the envelope and unfolded the letter. Then she began to cry.

"What's the matter?" asked Mrs. Eisenberg.

Sally's sobs got even louder. "It's from papa!"

## Comparison Shopping

Sadie Weintraub asked for two bagels.

"That'll be twenty cents, please," said the baker.

"Twenty cents!" exclaimed Sadie. "Why, that's ten cents a bagel! The man across the street only charges *six* cents!"

"So, buy them across the street," shrugged the baker.

"But they're all out of bagels across the street," said Sadie.

"Lady, when I'm all out of bagels, I only charge a nickel apiece."

**M**any wealthy men are known for their penurious habits. It is often said that millionaires make their money by watching every penny.

A cabbie once recognized Nathan Rothschild while driving the financier to his London home. When Rothschild alighted and paid his fare, the driver was disappointed to discover that the tip he received was quite small.

"You know, Mr. Rothschild," he said, "your daughter Julie gives me a much larger tip than that."

"That's all right for her," observed Rothschild dryly. "*She's* got a rich father."

## Relatively Speaking

A young man recently graduated from Yale took a job with a large clothing firm as a stockroom boy. He worked hard, and within a few months was made a salesman. In another six months he was promoted to sales manager, and soon afterwards to general manager.

A few days after his last promotion, he was called into the president's office. The president explained that he would retire soon and turn his position over to the young man.

The young man said, "Thanks."

"Thanks!" roared the president. "You've been with this firm only a year and already you're taking over the presidency. Is that all you can think of to say?"

"Well," amended the young man, "thanks a lot, Dad."

It was a fearful night. Lightning shot through the sky and the thunder roared in blasts that would frighten anybody. The rain came down in sheets.

The door of a little bakery opened and a drenched man came up to the counter and said, "Let me have two bagels."

The baker looked at him incredulously. "What," said the baker, "you came out on a night like this just for two bagels? That's all?"

"Yes, that's all," answered the man. "That's all I need. Just one for me and one for Pauline."

"Who's Pauline?" asked the baker.

"Oh what the hell difference is it to you?" answered the man. "Pauline is my wife. Who do you think she is? Would my mother send me out on a night like this?"

A successful self-made man was at the bank one day when he ran into an old school chum. "Well, if it ain't my old pal Walberg! How's by you?"

"Pretty good," said the friend. "By the way, I'm no longer Walberg. I changed my name to Eldridge."

The other man was surprised. "And where did you get the name 'Eldridge,' Schlomo?"

"What do you mean 'where'?" said the friend. "Don't you remember twenty years ago we both lived on Eldridge Street? Well, that's where I got the name. And what's more, I'm no more Schlomo. People now call me C.R."

His friend was even more curious. "And what does C.R. stand for?"

"C.R.—that stands for corner Rivington."

The partners had advertised for a bookkeeper. They agreed that Joe would do the interviewing. They sat expectantly outside Joe's office while Joe interviewed the first candidate. After a few minutes, Joe emerged and said: "Oh boy, is this girl a beaut! I asked her how much is two and two, and she said five. Of course she knows that two and two is four. What a sense of optimism! Imagine a bookkeeper who'll take the worst figures and turn them into the most glowing results. Boy, two and two, five, that's really something!"

The partners agreed.

After his next interview, Joe gave his report: "Well, this is also a pretty bright girl we have here. I asked her how much two and two was, and she said, 'Two and two?—that's three.' Now, that's a girl who is going to save us money."

The partners thought a moment, then one of them said: "You know, she seems a very conservative girl. We could use a girl like her."

Joe interviewed the next woman. Excitedly, he told the partners: "I asked her how much two and two was. She said: 'two and two, why, that's four.' You know, this one's really level-headed. She doesn't say five, she doesn't say three, she says four. She's got her two feet on the ground."

A perplexed partner looked at Joe and said: "Joe, you've really got a problem here.

Tell me: which one are you going to hire?"

"Ah," Joe replied, "That's easy. The one with the big tits."

Jake was lying in bed with Sadie, to whom he had been married for 12 years. On this particular night, Jake felt horny. "Sadie," he said, "lift up the nightgown."

Sadie didn't answer.

Jake tried once again. "Hey, Sadie, be a good girl. Lift up the nightgown."

Sadie still didn't answer.

Jake, furious, stormed out of the room, slamming the door.

In response to his outburst, Sadie locked the door.

For half an hour, Jake walked the living room floor. Then he strode back to the bedroom, pushed on the door, and found it was locked. Oh! So that was the way the wind was blowing. "Sadie," he pleaded, "open the door. I'm sorry I got sore. Open the door."

Sadie didn't answer.

Now Jake thundered, "Sadie, if you don't open the door, I swear I'll break it down!"

"You'll break it down?" replied Sadie. "Look at my athlete! A nightgown he can't lift up, and a door he'll break down!"

## Not a gigolo

A middle-aged man went to a middle-aged singles dance. After he had been standing alone for a half-hour, a woman approached him and said, "Would you like to dance?"

"A Fred Astaire I'm not," he answered, "but a little bit of dancing I'd like." So off they trotted to the dance floor.

After 20 minutes or so she said, "Would you care to have a drink?"

"A big-shot drinker I'm not," he said, "but one drink couldn't hurt." So off they went to the bar.

After half an hour's conversation, she said, "How about coming to my place?"

"A Romeo I'm not," he replied, "but a little romance can't hurt," so they left together.

The next morning, as he was about to leave, she said, "How about a little money?"

"A gigolo I'm not," he replied, "but a little money I'll take."

## I Admit It!

A peddler was brought to court by a cop who found him peddling without a license. While the peddler was sitting in the courtroom waiting his turn to appear before the bench, he listened to the proceedings of other cases.

A prostitute was brought up before the judge. The judge asked her, "What do you have to say?"

"Oh," she said, "I was minding my own business. I was standing in front of an attractive store window just looking at some shoes. Along came this cop, and said I was hustling."

"Well, were you?" said the judge.

"No, not at all. I'm absolutely innocent."

"Naturally," said the judge. "Your record proves that! You've been before this court six times this year. I fine you $100 and 30 days in the cooler."

The next woman, brought up on the same charge, again offered a lame excuse; and the judge, in a fury, fined her $250, with two months in jail.

The third girl arraigned said, "Your Honor, I was caught redhanded. I was soliciting. I have nothing more to say."

"Well," said the judge, "at least you're honest about it. I'll let you off with a $25 fine, and don't let it happen again."

Then the peddler was brought before the bench. "How do you plead?" asked the judge.

"Your Honor, what shall I tell you? You're a wise judge; you see through everything. Your honor, I'm guilty. I'm a whore!"

## Oh That Jaguar!

Max had been living with his shrewish wife for thirty years. But he couldn't stand the nagging any longer. He consulted his friend Shmuel about what to do.

"Why not do her in?" suggested Shmuel.

"If I do that I'll be thrown in jail. I don't want to spend the rest of my life in prison."

Shmuel considered, then he said, "Well, why don't you buy her a car? She can't drive. Maybe she'll have an accident, and her death won't be on your head."

So Max bought his wife a little sportscar. But when he met Shmuel a week later, he still looked sad. "She drives it perfectly," said Max. "I threw my money away."

Shmuel knew what was wrong. "That car you bought her was too small. Why don't you get her a large car that will be hard to handle? She's bound to get into an accident with a big sedan."

So Max bought his wife a huge Cadillac. But that didn't work either. "She drives that one perfectly, too," he told Shmuel a week later. "What do I do now?"

"Well, there's one other thing you can try. Splurge and get her a Jaguar."

When Shmuel ran into Max a week later, he was all smiles.

"So what happened? Shmuel asked him.

"Wonderful!" exclaimed Max. "One bite, and she was finished!"

## Not Heifetz

Jack Silvers wanted to entertain his mother, so he bought two front-row-center seats and accompanied her to the Barnum & Bailey Circus. His mother watched all the acts disdainfully. Nothing seemed to please her. She wasn't at all impressed by the lion tamer; the dancing elephants didn't amuse her; the tumblers left her cold. Then the main act was announced. Hidalgo would walk a tightrope fifty feet in the air while playing a violin.

Jack nudged his mother and said, "Ma, watch this. This is the big one. Don't be frightened. This is gonna be great!"

His mother didn't change her expression. To the applause of the crowd, the man walked across the tightrope playing one of Mozart's minuets in a manner worthy of a concert hall. Then, to everybody's amazement, he took one foot off the tightrope, and standing on tip-toe he played Beethoven's Moonlight Sonata.

Jack Silvers crowed, "Well, Ma, what do you say to that?"

"Well," conceded his mother, "okay . . . but a Heifetz he ain't."

## None Now

Greenstein and his family decided to move from New York to the Pacific Northwest.

"But what will you do there?" asked his friends.

"I'm strong," said Greenstein. "I'll be a lumberjack."

So the family moved West. Greenstein went out to look for a job as a lumberjack. The first foreman he met was impressed with his muscles, but wanted a physical demonstration of strength. He pointed to a tree with a twelve-inch trunk and asked Greenstein to cut it down. Greenstein did it in one minute.

"I can't believe it," said the astonished foreman. "My best cutter couldn't do that tree in less than four minutes! Please, Mr. Greenstein, do just one more so I know my eyes aren't deceiving me."

He pointed to a tree 16 inches thick. Greenstein downed it in two minutes.

"That's unbelievable, Mr. Greenstein. That tree would have taken any of my men ten minutes! Tell me, where did you work before this?"

"Well," said Greenstein modestly, "when I learned lumberjacking, I was in the Sahara."

"In the Sahara?" The foreman was incredulous. "But there are no trees in the Sahara!"

"Not any more there aren't."

## Not to Worry

Mrs. Gold fell asleep quickly one night, but her husband lay awake tossing and turning. Finally the commotion awoke Mrs. Gold, and she began complaining.

"Harry, what is it? Why are you tossing and turning so much that I can't even get a minute's sleep?"

"Oh, sweetheart," sighed Mr. Gold, "I'm so worried, that's what it is. I borrowed $3,000 dollars from Jake Stein across the street, and I thought business was going to get better, but it's worse. The note is due tomorrow, and I've no idea where I'm going to get the money to pay it with."

"Is that what's keeping you awake?" asked Mrs. Gold. And with that, she opened up the window and started screaming, "Jake! Jake!"

In half-a-minute, Jacob Stein was at his window. "What's the matter?" he yelled back.

"Jake," yelled Mrs. Gold, "Harry owes you three grand. The note is due tomorrow. He's been up all night worrying where to get the money, but he can't raise it. Now *you* worry!"

**W**hat do you call an uncircumcised Jewish baby?

*A girl.*

An eighty-year-old widower announced one day that he was taking a bride of twenty-three. Needless to say, his family was terribly distressed; they tried every means to dissuade him. But nothing worked.

So they appealed to their rabbi, a young man of rather liberal views. The rabbi promised to talk to the old man. But when he visited the prospective groom, he found his arguments were to no avail.

But the rabbi had a suggestion. Why not also take in a boarder? The rabbi reasoned that the old man would not be able to share his bride's youthful energy, and she would soon grow tired of his inertia. With a boarder, the young girl could still tend to her husband, while the young boarder would provide her with proper companionship.

It was a revolutionary concept, but it had merit. The old widower thought about it and agreed. "Sure, I get it," he said. "My family won't like it, but what business is it of theirs? If I am satisfied, why should they object? And the young lady, as you say, would be taken care of in the way of companionship, and so on."

The rabbi felt he'd done a good deed, and left for his summer vacation with a sense of accomplishment. When he returned, he went immediately to see how the newlyweds were doing.

"I want you to know we are both very happy," said the old man. "What's more, to the surprise of my family, my wife is pregnant."

"Oh," smiled the rabbi. "I suppose, then, you took in a young boarder as I suggested."

"Yes, I did," exclaimed the old man. "And she's pregnant, too."

## The Rabinowitz Curse

The new neighbor joined the mah jongg group for the first time, and all the ladies gaped at the huge diamond she wore.

"It's the third most famous diamond in the world," she told the women confidentially. "First is the Hope diamond, then the Kohinoor diamond, and then this one—the Rabinowitz diamond."

"It's beautiful!" admired one woman enviously. "You're so lucky!"

"Not so lucky as you think," the newcomer maintained. "Unfortunately, along with the famous Rabinowitz diamond, goes the famous Rabinowitz curse."

"And what is that?" wondered the women.

The woman heaved an enormous sigh. "Mr. Rabinowitz," she said.

## A Rose by Any Other Name

Sam Weinstein and Sol Applebaum owned a clothing factory and were quite pleased with the way business was going. One day, Sam decided that a well-to-do person ought to have a more elegant name. So he started calling himself Whittaker. And he changed the sign on the front of the factory from WEINSTEIN AND APPLEBAUM to WHITTAKER AND APPLEBAUM.

Sol was not to be outdone. He wanted to be elegant, too. So he also changed his name to Whittaker. Now the sign in front of the factory read WHITTAKER AND WHITTAKER.

One morning, a prospective buyer came to call. "I'd like to see Mr. Whittaker," the man had said.

"Which one?" asked the receptionist, "Weinstein or Applebaum?"

## When in Rome

A merchant moved down South from New York into one of the backwater towns. He seemed to be doing rather well, but then at about the beginning of April, the sales started to slacken very noticeably.

Sam Cohen pondered and pondered about the cause of the decline in business. Suddenly he realized, as he walked the streets, that every other establishment on Main Street had an Easter sign out front and that all the windows were especially dressed for the holiday.

Sam was in a quandary. He was a religious Jew—how could he, in good conscience, pay obeisance to Easter? He was up all night thinking. The next morning he arose and his face was beaming. He had worked out the solution.

That afternoon, Cohen's general store also contained an Easter sign. It read: "Christ is risen, but Cohen's prices are still the same."

## The Road to Riches

Morris had just started his new job as a bus driver and he approached his work conscientiously. For five straight days, his fares totaled a steady $75. No matter how diligent he was, he always ended the day with the same $75.

The following Monday, however, Morris proudly handed the company cashier a pouch containing $314. The bus official was astonished. "Fantastic!" he said. "How did you do it?"

"It was easy," explained Morris. "After five days on that cockamamy route, I figured business would *never* improve. So I drove over to 14th Street, and worked there. I tell you, that street is a gold mine!"

## You Can"t Fool Me!

Mr. Rosen had spent two weeks in New York City on business and was taking the train back to his suburban town. Sitting next to him on the train was a young man he didn't know. Since the train ride was long, Mr. Rosen decided to strike up a conversation.

"Where are you headed?" he asked.

The stranger smiled and said, "To Glens Falls."

Mr. Rosen was surprised. "Why, that's where I'm going! As a matter of fact, I live there! Is it a business trip?"

"No," said the young man, "it's social."

"Oh, do you have relatives there?"

"No, I don't."

Mr. Rosen thought a bit. "Are you married?" he asked.

"No, I'm not."

Now Rosen mused to himself. "He's going to Glens Falls, he's not married, it's not business, and he has no relatives there. So why is he going? Obviously, to meet a girl—to meet her family? Confirm their engagement? But who? There are only three Jewish families he could possibly know ... the Resnicks, the Feldsteins, and the Sanowitzes.

"It couldn't be the Resnicks, Resnick has only sons. The Feldsteins have two girls, but one's married, and the other's in college and she wouldn't be home at this time of year. It must be the Sanowitzes. They have three: Marsha, Rebekkah, and Rochelle. Marsha is already engaged. Becky is too plump and unattractive for this nice-looking young man. So it must be Rochelle. Yes, Rochelle! She's beautiful!"

With this, Mr. Rosen broke his silence and smiled at the stranger. "Well, congratulations on your forthcoming marriage to Rochelle Sanowitz!"

"But—but how did you know?" stammered the young man.

"Why, it's obvious!" answered Mr. Rosen.

Have you heard of the Jewish nymphomaniac?

No matter what, she has to have a man at least once a month.

And of the Jewish drop-out?

He quit school after he got his Master's.

A young girl was taking the State Board examination to become a nurse. The doctor asked her, "How do you wash genitals?"

"The same way you wash Jews!" she replied.

## Keeping Up with the Cohens

To celebrate little Howie's bar mitzvah, Mr. and Mrs. Shapiro sought something unique. The usual catered affairs were a thing of the past. All year long, Howie's friends had been having miniature-golf bar mitzvahs, amusement-park bar mitzvahs, and Broadway-show bar mitzvahs. For weeks, the Shapiros racked their brains trying to come up with something that hadn't been done before.

Finally Mr. Shapiro decided. "We'll have a safari bar mitzvah! Hang the expense! We'll charter a plane for all our friends and relatives and fly to the depths of the jungle."

All the arrangements were made. Soon the great day came. Led by a native African guide, the bar mitzvah party made its way along the safari trail.

They had only been hiking a few minutes when the guide came to an abrupt halt. Impatiently, Mr. Shapiro asked, "What's happened? Why are we stopping?"

The guide replied, "We'll have to wait here for awhile. There are two more bar mitzvahs right ahead of us."

## In the Swim

Two bankers, Morris and Harry, decided to take

a vacation together and get away from it all. They rented a cabin on a lake so they could go fishing.

The first morning of their vacation, the pair got into the boat and made their way out into the middle of the lake. Suddenly a large motorboat sped by, and the force of its wake caused the smaller craft to capsize.

"Help me, Morris! I can't swim very well." shouted Harry.

Morris could swim, but the problem was that Harry was twice his size. He'd never be able to rescue him. So he hollered, "I'll go get help. Do you think you can float alone?"

Harry was indignant. "Morris, how can you talk about business at a time like this?"

## Payoff

In the days of pioneering the wild old West, Jake and Izzy were traveling through Colorado by stagecoach. Suddenly the coach stopped, and Jake realized that robbers were about to stage a hold-up.

Quickly, Jake took some money from his wallet and handed it to his companion. "Izzy," he explained, "here is the fifty dollars I owe you."

Steve and Ralph had been partners for many, many years. Sudenly, out of the blue, Steve announced one day, "Listen, Ralph, you're going to have to find a new partner; I'm leaving."

"Leaving—for Heaven's sakes, why?

"Don't ask me; I'd rather not say, but I'm going."

"Listen, we've been together for eight years. You can't just walk out like this. You owe me some little explanation, at least."

"OK, if you insist. I've just had it with you. I've taken it for as long as I can stand, and now I can't take one more second with you."

"Had it? Had what? What are you talking about?"

"Well, if you insist, here it is: I've taken the crap too long. Not one simple word comes out of you. Everything is so pretentious, so affected.

"Affected? Pretentious? Who's affected? Moi?

## Horse Player

A horse player was recounting his doleful experiences at the track. "I had a very strange dream the other night. I kept dreaming about hats—all kinds of hats—men's hats, women's hats, witches' hats, big hats, little hats, hats, hats, hats. I decided the dream must be telling me something. So the next day I went to Bowie to try out my hunch. I bet on every horse that had a name that had something to do with hats. In the first race, I put 50 bucks on Fedora, and she came in first. The second race, I put 100 bucks on Straw Hat, and she beat the field by three lengths. Seeing I was on a winning streak, I put 500 bucks on a nag called Blue Bonnet in the third race, and sure enough, she won by a nose. In the fourth race, I couldn't find any horse with a hat name but I felt like a winner so I put all my winnings plus another $250 on a horse called Foul Play, and she dragged in seventh in a field of eight."

"Too bad," said his friend. "By the way, who won that race?"

"Oh," he said, "some mare with the crazy name of Yarmulka."

## Quick Settlement

Abe Seltzer was passing a golf course when he was struck in the head by a golf ball.

Seething, Abe picked up the ball and gestured wildly at the player running anxiously toward him. "I'll sue you in court for five hundred dollars!" Abe shouted angrily.

The golfer tried to excuse himself. "I hollered 'Fore!' " he said.

"All right!" answered Abe, "I'll take it."

## Footloose and Fancy Free

The limousine pulled up in front of one of New York's poshest hotels and the doorman sprang forward to hold open the car door for Mrs. Henrietta de Rothsberg. Immediately, Mrs. de Rothsberg called for half a dozen bellboys.

The boys came running, and the lady dispatched them one by one with her suitcases, hatboxes, and wig stands. When she came to the last one, she announced regally, "And you, you can carry my son Steven."

The bellboy was aghast. Steven was a teenager, and no scrawny chicken. "But, madam," he complained, "surely the young man can walk."

Mrs. de Rothsberg was adamant. "Of course he can walk!" she explained. "But, thanks be to God, he'll never have to."

## Tears From a Stone

It was at a country fair. Onto a platform there strode a huge giant of a man. He grabbed a 500-pound barbell and, with ease, lifted it above his head. For his next feat, he kneeled under a piano on which heavy weights had been distributed and, after tensing his muscles, he slowly raised the piano aloft on his back.

The hawker then came forward and announced, "For his next feat Lionel Strongfellow will perform a unique stunt. Here is a lemon, an ordinary, fresh lemon. Lionel Strongfellow will squeeze every bit of juice out of this lemon using both hands. If anybody in this audience can squeeze another drop of juice out of this lemon after Lionel Strongfellow has handled it, we will award the lucky man a prize of $500."

Strongfellow then took the lemon and-squeezed it into a pulpy mass. He kneaded it again and again with both hands until it seemed that there wasn't any juice left in it at all. Then, in response to the hawker's invitation, three powerful men from the audience came up and each in turn tried to extract a drop of juice out of the lemon. None succeeded.

The hawker asked, "Anyone else care to try?" A slight, short man strode up to the stage. It looked like sheer folly, but the little fellow took the lemon, squeezed it, and out spouted a stream of juice.

The hawker gave the man the prize and asked in amazement, "Tell me, sir, by what kind of legerdemain, by what kind of magic, by what kind of incredible strength were you able to get juice out of this lemon, where everyone else before had failed?"

The man looked up and said, "Well, I've had lots of experience. You see, I've been a collector for the United Jewish Appeal for 12 years."

## Where The Best Is None Too Good

Mrs. Kohansky went to her butcher of many years and said, "Bernie, today I need a beautiful chicken, maybe four pounds."

Bernie pointed out three chickens on the display counter, but Mrs. Kohansky turned up her nose at all of them. "I asked for a *beautiful* chicken," she sniffed.

So Bernie went to the back of the store, and from his refrigerator room he extracted an especially plump fowl. He brought it forward with pride.

The lady was cautious. She took the chicken and slowly began to examine each part with her fingers—lifting the wings, feeling the breast, and groping inside the cavity.

Finally, the butcher's patience waned. "Tell me, Mrs. Kohansky," he demanded, "do you think *you* could pass such a test?"

## Kosher!

A Jewish mental patient was causing quite a stir in the institution because he wouldn't eat the food.

"I'm kosher!" shouted Moskowitz. "I won't eat this food. I want kosher meals!"

So the staff hired a Jewish woman from the community to cook special kosher meals for

Moskowitz. Everybody was envious, for Moskowitz's meals were much that theirs weren't.

Friday night rolled around, and Moskowitz pushed back his chair after a delicious chicken dinner, and lit up a big black cigar. This was too much for the director, who called Moskowitz into his office.

"Now see here, Moskowitz. You're getting away with murder. You get the best meals because you claim you only eat kosher food. And now, on Friday night, on your Sabbath, you flout your religion, and smoke a cigar!"

Moskowitz merely shrugged his shoulders. "Why are you arguing with me? I'm crazy, ain't I?"

## Can You Beat It?

Sadie wasn't feeling well, and she knew she should see a doctor. So she asked her friend Becky the name of the doctor she used.

"His name's Feinstein," said Becky, "but you should know he's expensive."

"How expensive is expensive?"

"Well, it's fifty dollars for the first visit, and twenty-five for every visit after that."

Sadie went off to see Dr. Feinstein. She smiled brightly and said to the nurse, "Hi, honey. Here I am again!"

Jake and his wife had been living together happily for many years. One day, one of his friends asked him how it was that he and his wife never quarreled.

"Well," answered Jake, "we have an arrangement. She makes all the small decisions, and I make all the big decisions."

"How does that work? What do you mean?"

"Well, when it comes to such small routine matters as to where we should live, where we should go on vacations, what school the kids should attend, things like that, she has the final say."

"And?" queried his friend.

"When it comes to the big fundamental questions like should the United States declare war on Iran? Should Congress appropriate a sum for travel to Mars? Or who should be elected mayor of New York? On all big things like that, I have the final say."

Mrs. Ginsberg, nearing 75, wasn't feeling too good, and on advice of friends, decided to visit Dr. Kantrowitz, a gynecologist.

Towards the end of her examination, she turned to the doctor and said, "Such a nice young man. Does your mother know how you're making a living?"

**A** businessman was sitting quietly in a fine restaurant eating his lunch when suddenly a stranger hailed him.

"Hey there, Poznanski!" shouted the man. "My goodness, what happened to you? You used to be short, and now you're tall. You used to be blond, and now you're dark-haired. You used to have blue eyes, and now they're brown!"

The businessman was polite but firm. "I beg your pardon, sir, but I'm not Poznanski."

"My God!" exclaimed the other. "You changed your name, too!"

## The Awful Truth

The president of the congregation had to undergo surgery. The board met to decide how to show their concern. Finally, it was agreed that the secretary of the congregation would visit the president in the hospital.

Two days after the operation, the secretary visited the sickroom. "I bring you the good wishes of our board," he said. "We hope you get well and live to be 120 years old!"

The president smiled back weakly.

"And that's an official resolution," continued the secretary, "passed by a vote of twelve to nine."

It was the first day of school and the teacher was anxious to get to know her class and have them learn about each other as well. So she suggested that as she called out each name, the child would stand at his seat and say any sentence that came into mind.

She started with Tommy Avery. Tommy stood and said, "I like to play baseball."

"Good," said the teacher. "Now John Bennett."

"I like the summertime because then I can go to camp."

"Harold Cohen."

"I pledge a hundred dollars."

## Mind Your Own Business

Izzy thought he saw his friend Tannenbaum walking up ahead of him on the street, so he quickened his pace and clapped the man soundly on the back. "Tannenbaum! I haven't seen you in a long time!" he cried.

Startled, the man turned around. He wasn't Tannenbaum at all. And he was pretty irritated at being thumped on the back. "My name is not Tannenbaum!" he fairly shouted. "And what's the idea of giving me such a hard slap?"

Izzy retreated icily. "What business is it of yours what I do to Tannenbaum?"

Mr. Gold had been married for many years when he had to go to Paris for a business trip. In that city of love, he easily fell victim to the amorous advances of the pretty mademoiselles.

But somehow Mrs. Gold found out about it. She wired her husband at his hotel: "COME HOME! WHY SPEND MONEY THERE FOR WHAT YOU CAN GET HERE FOR FREE?"

The next day, she received a cable in reply: "I KNOW YOU AND YOUR BARGAINS!"

## The Halcyon Days

Mrs. Rosen was at a hotel in the Catskills, sunning herself by the pool, when a group of ladies asked if she would like to join them in a game of mah jongg. Mrs. Rosen was delighted.

So the ladies began to play, apparently welcoming Mrs. Rosen into their circle. But suddenly, one of the women raised a hand to gain everyone's attention.

"I think we ought to inform Mrs. Rosen about our rules for conversation," she said. "Mrs. Rosen, there are some subjects we never discuss. We never discuss husbands: they are all miserable. We never discuss fur coats: they are all gorgeous. We never discuss grandchildren: they are all geniuses. And we never discuss sex. What was, was."

One veteran of Miami Beach had been coming every winter for twenty years. One day, she spotted an old friend from New York on the beach.

"Sadie!" she called out. "It's so good to see you! How are you?"

"Molly!" cried the other. "Actually I'm not feeling so good. That's why I came down here for a week."

Molly thought for a minute, and then she asked discreetly, "Darling, have you been through the menopause yet?"

Sadie looked at her. "The Menopause? I told you I just arrived. I haven't even been through the Fountainbleau yet!"

## No News Is No Noose

Two partners in the garment industry were having business problems; it looked as if they might have to declare bankruptcy. But at the brink, a particular line of dresses seemed to lure a buyer. A West Coast outlet wanted to buy the whole line, at a price which would put the partners well into the black. The partners were overjoyed.

"The only thing is," warned the buyer, "I have to have the deal approved by the home office. I'm sure they'll agree, but I do have to check with them. I'm going back tomorrow. If you don't hear from me by Friday closing time, you can be sure everything's okay."

The week went by slowly; and Friday crawled. The two men sat without moving at their desks, unable to concentrate on any kind of work. Without this deal, they would definitely go under. They sweated the hours out, minute by minute.

Two o'clock went by, three o'clock, then four o'clock, and now they were close to pay dirt. Four-thirty came, and they were holding their breath. Suddenly, a messenger burst into the office. "Telegram!" he said. The men froze in terror.

Finally, one of the partners stood up. Slowly he opened the telegram, and read it quickly.

Then came a shriek of joy. "Harry! Good news! Your brother died!"

## Tie One On

For his birthday, Mrs. Finkelstein gave her grown-up son Charlie two Dior ties. One was red and the other blue.

On his next visit to his mother, Charlie put on the red tie and strode into the apartment.

His mother took one look at him and sighed, "Ah! The blue one you didn't like."

Young Samuel arrived home after his first day at Hebrew school.

"Well," said his mother, "tell me what you learned today."

"Today we learned all about Moses," answered Samuel.

"And what do you know about Moses?"

"Well, he was this general, see. And he got all the Jews together in formation and marched them out of Egypt, with General Pharaoh's Egyptians hot on their trail. And then in front of him, there was the Red Sea blocking his path. So Moses ordered bombs dropped, and bang! The waters parted just long enough for the Jews to get across. And when the Egyptians followed, they were all drowned."

The mother was aghast. "Is that how they teach the story of Moses nowadays?"

"No, Mom," answered Sammy. "But if I told you the story the way the teacher told it to us, you'd never believe it."

For years, Jake had been itching to have a little kooky sex. He wanted a little thrill. But Becky had steadfastly refused to humor him.

One day, Jake brought home a gorgeous mink coat. He said, "Becky, try it on."

She wrapped herself in that beautiful garment, paraded up and down in front of the mirror, and fell in love with the coat.

"That coat," declared Jake, "costs all of $12,000. Do you want it?"

"Oh, do I want it!" said Becky.

"Okay, if you want it, you got to do what I want for once! We've got to have sex—just once—like the dogs do it."

Becky was taken aback, and then looked at the coat longingly. "Okay, Jake," she said. "I'll give in. Just once. But Jake, dear, not on our block!"

**A** non-Jew was walking down the street on a sunny day in September when he saw a crowd of people standing outside a building. It was the Jewish New Year, and the building was a synagogue.

When he came nearer, the man saw that everyone was dressed in his or her finest clothing. Intrigued, he wandered into the building.

There, he met the rabbi, who looked splendid dressed in white and gold. "What kind of a show do you have here?" asked the passerby. "It is good?"

"It should be," answered the rabbi. "It has been running for nearly six thousand years."

## Timing is Everything

Izzy's friend Yosef said he had found a parrot that not only could speak, but could speak Hebrew. Izzy was skeptical, but when he went to Yosef's house, they put a yarmulke on the bird's head, and the parrot immediately recited the full Friday night services.

Izzy was amazed, and begged his friend to let him buy the bird. After much cajoling, Yosef agreed. For the price of ten dollars, Izzy was able to take away the *dovvining* bird.

On Rosh Hashonah, Izzy took his bird to the synagogue. He passed the word around that his parrot could sing the prayers. Everyone laughed at his pretensions, and he extracted wagers of 10 to 1 that his bird couldn't follow the service for even three minutes.

When the prayers began, Izzy put a yarmulke on the parrot's head and commanded him to sing. But the bird was silent.

"Go, pray, like you did for Yosef," Izzy urged. But the parrot wouldn't open its beak.

"Pray, you numbskull! I have a bet on you!" But the parrot wouldn't utter a sound. Finally, Izzy had to admit defeat, and left the synagogue downcast and deep in debt.

When he got home, he lashed into the bird. "So you shame me in front of everybody, eh? So you make me lose ten to one bets? So you pretend you don't know how to pray? Why did you do that?"

Finally, the parrot spoke up. "Don't be stupid!" said the parrot. "Comes Yom Kippur, you'll make a killing!"

The teacher in a tenement district sent Mrs. Cohen a candid note which read:

"Your son Abie stinks. Give him a bath."

Mrs. Cohen's reply was just as direct. "My son Abie ain't no rose. Don't smell him. Learn him."

A man took his family to a kosher restaurant. They were surprised when their waiter turned out to be Chinese! What's more, the Chinaman took their orders in Yiddish and even addressed them in Yiddish. The family was impressed.

When they had finished their meal, the man asked to see the manager.

"The food was excellent," he said. "I compliment you. But how did you get a Chinese waiter to talk Yiddish so well?"

"Shh!" said the proprietor. "Don't let him hear you. He thinks he's learning English!"

Lenny and Mildred had been having marital difficulties, so they repaired to a marriage counselor. At the session, Lenny complained that Mildred didn't prepare proper meals for him. Mildred's complaint was that Lenny hadn't been fulfilling his conjugal obligations. After much altercation, the marriage counselor straightened things out; the final verdict was that Milly was to go to cooking school, and Lenny was to sleep with Milly semi-annually.

Going down the stairs, from the office, Milly, was glowing with satisfaction. As they reached the street, however, a troubling thought struck her. She took Lenny by the hand, looked up into his eyes, and said: "Tell me, Lenny, how many times a week is semi-annually?"

Fred Tannenbaum was stationed in a small Southern town. There he met a girl and fell madly in love. He called his mother to tell her he wanted to get married. Yes, the girl was Jewish.

"But you must be married by a rabbi!" insisted Mrs. Tannenbaum.

"There aren't any rabbis around here!" said Fred.

"I'll send you one!"

And so Mrs. Tannenbaum set off for her Lower East Side shul. She pleaded with her old rabbi to go South with her to marry her son. And he agreed. For the occasion, the rabbi put on his best beaver hat, his favorite black silk wedding suit, and his long black frock coat that almost touched the ground.

When they got off the plane, Mrs. Tannenbaum showed the cab driver the girl's address, but somehow or other he dropped them at the wrong place and drove off. Mrs. Tannenbaum, with the rabbi in tow, walked up and down the streets searching for Freddie and his bride-to-be. And as they went along, they seemed to attract a growing following. By the time they found the right address, there were a dozen people behind them staring at the rabbi.

The rabbi pulled himself up to his full height and faced the crowd of gaping Southerners. "What's the matter?" he said. "Ain't you never seen before a Yankee?"

Sam Ginsburg got up to answer his phone. A very British voice asked "Is this Stoner Wellington Cadwallader?"

"Oy!" answered Sam, "Have you got a wrong number!"

Molly and Yetta were in the middle of their once-a-month telephone call for keeping up-to-date on each other's gossip.

"Oh, and Molly," said Yetta, "did I tell you about my son David?"

"No, what about David?" asked Molly.

"He is going to a psychiatrist!" said the mother proudly. "Twice a week he goes to a psychiatrist!"

Molly knew she was supposed to be impressed, but she didn't really understand why. "Is that good?" she asked.

"Of course it's good!" exclaimed Yetta. "Fifty dollars an hour he pays, fifty dollars! And all he talks about is me!"

There was a young reform rabbi whose hobby was golf. Having a large congregation, however, he didn't often have time to relax. He missed playing very badly.

So the rabbi searched his calendar and found that he had only one free day—and not another for the next six months! But that day was a Saturday. Could he dare slip off after services on this one day for his favorite sport? The rabbi decided quickly, mumbled an apology to God, and on Saturday drove off to a course thirty miles away hoping to play unrecognized.

Up in heaven, an angel looked down, and to

his horror, he noticed who was on the golf course. Immediately, God was notified and asked what should be done.

God was greatly saddened. He leaned out of heaven, and with a mighty force, blew a strong gust of wind straight down onto the golf course. The rabbi was on the second hole when the heavenly breeze caught up with him, and that gust took the ball from the tee just as the rabbi swung. Up went the ball, straight down the fairway to make a miraculous hole in one. The angel was aghast.

"But why did you do that, Lord? Is that what you call a punishment?"

The Holy One smiled. "Think about it," said God. "Who can he tell?"

Nate and Becky were spending a Sunday at the amusement park. They were having a lovely time. Then Nate decided to buy tickets for the tunnel of love.

The ride was slow and pleasant. When they emerged into the light, Becky smoothed down her dress, dabbed on her lipstick, and smiled shyly at Nate. She said demurely, "Nate, you know, you shouldn't have did it."

Nate turned to her and insisted: "I *didn't* did it."

Becky was flabbergasted. "What! *You* didn't did it? Well then, who *did* did it?"

The teacher entered her classroom in the school on Delancey Street and was horrified to find a small puddle on the floor right next to her desk.

"Who did this?" she demanded. No one spoke.

"I want to know who made this puddle," she said insistently. "Please raise your hand, whoever did it." Again, no child moved.

So she realized that the offender might be too embarrassed to confess and decided to try another tactic. She took a rag from the closet and left it on her desk. Then she said, "I'm going to leave the room for a few minutes. I want the person who made that puddle to clean it up while I'm gone."

She left the room, closing the door behind her, and after waiting five minutes, she again entered the classroom. But to her amazement, there were now *two* puddles near her desk! She was furious! Trying to compose herself and to figure out what to do next, she turned her back to the class and faced the blackboard.

And there, scrawled in big letters, she read: "The Phantom Pisher Strikes Again!"

## The Music Lover

For years, the boys had had a poker game

every Saturday night. Then, one Saturday, Mike Ginsberg said he wouldn't be able to play next Saturday because on that night the great pianist Shapiro was playing. The excuse was accepted.

Three weeks later, Ginsberg, at the close of the regular Saturday night game, said he'd be absent the following week. Asked why, he replied, "Well, Shapiro is playing that night."

The same thing happened two or three more times during the next few months, and finally one of the boys lost patience and confronted Mike. "Hey, look," he said, "since when have you become such a great music lover? Every time Shapiro is playing, does that mean that you gotta go and hear him?"

"Ah, no," rejoined Mike. "But when Shapiro's playing, that's the night I can go and see his wife."

**O**ne day, Mr. James Solomon bumped into Becky the Whore on 23rd Street. "Gee, Becky," he said, "I haven't seen you for a dog's age. Where've you been?"

"Oh," she said, "I've been up here on 23rd Street for the last two years. You see, when my daughter Sadie got married, I gave her 14th Street for a wedding present."

## O My! O My!

A man lay in bed in a hospital ward. Three doctors approached him and asked him what he was in the hospital for. The patient replied that he wanted to be castrated. The doctors looked at him askance, and said in unison, "What!"

He insisted: "Yes, I want to be castrated."

The operation was performed. After a few days, the patient was dressed and on his way out of the hospital when he passed the maternity ward, and saw a small crowd gathered in a room. He asked the nurse what was going on. "Oh," she said, "A little baby boy is being circumcised."

"Circumcised! he exclaimed. "Damn it! That's the word I meant."

**S**am Goldstein had never been to a show in the legitimate theater. For his birthday, his children decided to give him a present of a ticket for the Jewish theater.

The night after the show, they came to visit him and asked him eagerly what he thought of the show. "Ach," he answered, "it was simply nonsense. When she was willing, he wasn't willing. And when he was willing, she wasn't willing. And when they both were willing, down came the curtain."

An elderly lady consulted a psychologist. She complained that her husband was losing his potency.

The doctor asked "How old are you, Mrs. Finkel?"

"Seventy nine," she replied.

"And your husband? continued the doctor.

"He's eighty four."

"When did you first notice his impotence?" asked the doctor.

"Last night," replied Mrs. Finkel, "and I noticed it again this morning."

## Koolaid

Izzy was driving through the countryside when he became very thirsty. So in the next town, he looked for a coffee shop. But he found only a general store that was a combination hardware store, drugstore, and farmers' supply outlet all in one. Still, it boasted a soda fountain, so Izzy went in.

At the counter, he asked boldly, "Do you handle fertilizer here?"

"Why, yes," said the man, "I'll be glad to show you—"

"Never mind!" interrupted Izzy. "Just wash your hands, and make me a malted!"

**A** rabbi and a priest were talking one day They were longtime friends and knew each other well.

"Tell me," said the priest, "have you ever tasted ham? Be truthful now."

"Well," the rabbi became uncomfortable, "once, when I was in college. Curiosity became too much for me and I had a ham sandwich." The priest smiled benevolently.

"But now you tell me," the rabbi queried, "and be truthful, did you ever, perhaps, make love to a girl—"

Then the priest began to stammer. "Well, once, when I was in college, *before* I was ordained . . ." he sputtered.

The pair were quiet for a moment. Then the rabbi smiled. "It's better than ham, isn't it?"

## Who Can Disagree?

Boris Tomashefsky was probably the best-known actor on the Jewish stage. He really packed them in.

One night, during a performance toward the end of his career, Tomashefsky failed to appear for the third act. An announcer came to the stage and said, "Ladies and gentlemen, I have very sad news for you. Mr. Tomashefsky has just suffered a heart attack and cannot continue."

A voice from the gallery cried out, "Give him an enema."

The announcer then stepped forward, closer to the audience, and said, "My dear sir, perhaps you have not understood. Mr. Tomashefsky has just passed away."

Again the voice rang out, in raucous tones, "Give him an enema."

The announcer then said, "I know it's very shocking news, and I'm very sorry to have to be the one to announce it. But Mr. Tomashefsky is dead. Your suggestion could not possibly help him."

And the voice shot back, louder and more insistent, "Can't hurt."

After the United States launched its space program, the astronauts became overnight heroes. Everyone spoke of their accomplishments.

Two feisty Jewish ladies were indulging in their morning chat and one remarked, "Bessie, did you hear about the astronauts? I understand they went around the world several times!"

The other lady was not impressed. "Big deal!" she sniffed. "If you have money, you can afford to travel."

Billy Sperling came to his father and told him he was going to be married. The father, of course, asked to whom. Billy replied that his light of love was Mary McGrath, who lived down the street.

His father objected.

"Why are you marrying an Irish girl?" he asked.

"Well," Billy answered, "because Jewish girls complain all the time; they get sick all the time; they have stomach trouble all the time. You have to send them to a dentist four times a year. They have foot trouble, and they complain, and complain, and complain. When they have a child they scream."

The father answered, "Billy, do you mean to tell me that Irish girls don't complain, don't get sick, don't have other troubles, and that shiksas don't scream when they give birth?"

"Of course," said Billy, "but if a shiksa screams, who cares?"

"Papa, was Adam Jewish?"

"I'd say he was," answered the father.

"Tell me, Pop, was Eve Jewish?"

"Of course, my son. Who else but a Jewish girl would say to a man, 'Here, have a piece of fruit.'"

Little Herbie's parents decided he was of an age where they should start guarding their conversation.

When Aunt Dottie came to visit, she said to Herbie, "Well, young man, what's new around here?"

Herbie's reply was brief. "Who knows?" said the little boy. "They spell everything!"

When Nasser was visiting New York City in order to attend a meeting at the United Nations, he spent one afternoon seeing the sights of the city.

It happened that the Egyptian President was down by the East River when he leaned over too far and fell in. Hearing the holler for help, a fourteen-year-old boy came running. With some strenuous tugging, he was able to pull the Egyptian out of the water.

"I owe my life to you," said Nasser. "What is your name?"

"My name is Israel Cohen, Mr. Nasser."

"Oh, you know who I am?"

"Yes, sir."

"I'm very grateful to you. I'll give you anything you want or do anything you wish."

The boy didn't think twice. "I want just one thing. Please don't tell my father!"

## Blind Date

Sam was already in his twenties and he had never had a date with a girl, so his older brother decided it was time to do something about it. He arranged a blind date for Sam with a nice young girl who was just as innocent as Sammy. But he was very nervous. His hands became clammy and his tongue felt stiff as marble.

"Help me, Moish. I don't know how to talk to girls. How can I be a good conversationalist like you?" asked Sam.

Moish had some advice to offer. "Listen, Sam," he said, "I have a formula that never fails. Talk about family, food, and philosophy. Any of those topics is guaranteed to get a girl talking. Try it! I'm sure it'll work."

So Sam went to meet the girl. She was pretty and shy. Sam wanted very much to make a good impression. He thought of his brother's advice. First, he'd talk family.

"Tell me," he began nervously, "do you have a brother?"

"No!" came the girl's swift reply.

"Oh." Sam was stymied, so he moved to the topic of food. "Do you like noodles?"

"No!" she said again.

But Sam wasn't at a loss. He remembered his brother's advice. He'd talk philosophy. "Say," he said, "if you had a brother, would he like noodles?"

Finkel spent all morning trying to contact Saperstein and Shapiro, an important account. But when he asked for Saperstein, the secretary told him the man was out. And when he asked for Shapiro, the secretary told him he was tied up.

He'd called back five times, and finally had enough. "What kind of business is this?" he fumed. "One partner's out all morning, and the other's tied up for hours on end. What's going on there?"

The secretary apologized. "I'm sorry, Mr. Finkel, but, you see, whenever Mr. Saperstein goes out, he ties Mr. Shapiro up."

Two acquaintances were discussing business.

"You know," said Shapiro, "two months ago a big fire destroyed my business in Florida, and everything turned to ashes. All my assets were gone. If it were not that I carried a half million dollars in insurance, I would be a ruined man."

"You know," said Ginsberg, "it's a strange coincidence, but the same thing happened to me. About three months ago my shop in Key Largo was struck by a hurricane. Fortunately, I carried *double* insurance. That was my lifesaver. I got enough money to open up a new business here in New York."

"Great!" cried Shapiro, "but how does one go about arranging for a hurricane?"

## A Father's Woes

A much-loved rabbi died a peaceful death, and his soul rose swiftly to heaven.

There, the rabbi was warmly greeted by hosts of angels. They wanted to honor him by dressing him in finery and escorting him through the golden streets, for he had been such a fine man. But the rabbi, inexplicably, wouldn't participate. He covered his face with his hands, and fled from the midst of the celebrations.

Astonished, the angels brought the rabbi before God himself. "My child," said the Lord, "it is on record that you have lived entirely in accord with My wishes, and yet you refuse the honors that have, most fittingly, been prepared for you. Why?"

"Oh, Most Holy One," replied the rabbi, prostrating himself, "I am not as deserving as You think. Somewhere along the way I must have sinned, for my son, heedless of my example and of my precepts, turned Christian."

"Alas, I understand entirely and I forgive," said God. "I had the same trouble myself."

Billy Gold was having a little trouble with his Hebrew lessons, so his father decided to ask the rabbi if he could give him some personal attention.

After several months of private tutoring, Billy was doing a little better, but the only Hebrew he had mastered were the first few words of the Kaddish, the prayer said for the soul of a departed parent.

Approaching the rabbi anxiously, Mr. Gold said, "I wanted you to teach him some Hebrew, that's true, but why right away the prayer for the dead? Do I look so old to you? Do you think I'm going to die any minute?"

The rabbi explained calmly, "Mr. Gold, you should only live as long as it will take your son to learn the Kaddish."

## I'd Like to Try!

Some years ago, two rabbis met for lunch. After conducting a heavy philosophical exchange, the two turned to lighter topics.

"So," said one, "what do you think? One of our boys got to marry that Elizabeth Taylor!"

"Oh!" snapped the other, "It won't last a year!"

The first rabbi sighed. "I should have such a year!"

Three old Jews were sitting around drinking tea and philosophizing about life. One said, "You know, it is my opinion that the best thing there is in life is good health. Without good health, life isn't worth a darn."

The second took exception. "Well," he said, "I've known plenty of rich men who were sick, terribly sick. But they had lots and lots of money and they went to the best specialists. They went through all kinds of treatments and operations and they came out almost as good as new. The fact is that without money life isn't worth much. You can be as robust as a lion and still be miserable if you don't have a red cent. On the other hand, with money you can buy practically anything. In my opinion, the best thing in life is to have money."

The third one had listened patiently. And now he demurred, saying, "Yes, health is good, and money is good, but I've seen people with plenty of money who are utterly miserable, and I've seen people in good health who were miserable. The fact is that rich or poor, healthy or sick, life in itself is an enormous overwhelming misery. In my opinion, the best thing in life really is not to be born at all."

The other two responded to this remark by plunging themselves into deep contemplation. Finally, one broke the silence. "Yes, Danny, you're right. The best thing in life, as you say, is not to be born at all. But, tell me, who can be so lucky, one out of a million?"

## Lox

A schnorrer made his monthly call at Baron Rothschild's mansion and begged to be seen by the master. Admitted to the library, the schnorrer asked the tycoon to give him double his regular stipend, spilling out a heart-rending tale of woe.

Rothschild was moved, and gave the beggar what he had asked for. Yet the baron was suspicious, and commanded a servant to follow the poor man to see what he did with the money. The beggar headed for a swank delicatessen shop and spent the money on a lox.

The next month when the schnorrer came again to ask for more money, Rothschild erupted in anger.

"You scoundrel!" he cried, "What a trumped up hard luck story you handed me! As soon as you left my house last month, you went and spent the entire sum of money I gave you on lox!"

The schnorrer looked pitiful. "Ah, Baron," he replied, "put yourself in my position. When I haven't got money, I can't buy lox. When I have money, I can't buy lox. Tell me, your honor, when can I buy lox?"

## Answer That!

Mrs. Rosenbush was negotiating for a mink stole at Mendelovitch's. She asked a lot of questions.

"If I buy the coat and I get caught in the rain," she asked the salesman, "will it get ruined?"

"Look, lady," answered Mendelovitch, "did you ever see a mink carrying an umbrella?"

Minnie had been depressed, so she decided to try going to a psychiatrist. Perhaps he would do her some good. She made an appointment with Dr. Oglethorpe, recommended by her family doctor.

After one session with Minnie, Dr. Oglethorpe realized that the usual methods wouldn't work. So he said to her, "With your permission, I'd like to try something somewhat different. I'm going to leave the room for half an hour, and I want you to lie here on this couch and think about sex. Nothing else, just sex. When I come back, we'll talk about it."

The doctor left the room for half an hour, and when he returned, he sat down next to her with pencil and pad. "So, Minnie, tell me what you've been thinking about."

"All I could think of," said Minnie, "is that, at least for me, Seks—even though it's on Fifth Avenue—can't compare with Macy's."

Mr. and Mrs. Leibenstein had saved a lot of money and were traveling to a place they had always dreamed of—Hawaii.

But while on the plane to that exotic spot, the couple got into an argument over the pronunciation of the name. The wife insisted it was said with a "w"; the husband was sure the "w" was pronounced as a "v." They decided to ask a native as soon as they landed.

The plane pulled into the airport, the stairs were lowered, and the passengers debarked to the sounds of beautiful Hawaiian music being strummed for their welcome. Mr. and Mrs. Leibenstein approached one of the musicians and asked him, "Do you pronounce your island 'Hawaii' or 'Havaii'?"

"Havaii," said the man.

"Well, thank you," said Mr. Leibenstein, and he smiled smugly.

"You're velcome," said the musician.

## Depends How You Look at It

Two garment manufacturers met in the bank one Friday morning.

"So, Stanley," said one, "how's business?"

The other man just shrugged. "Ehhh," he said.

The first one smiled. "Well, for this time of the year, that's not bad!"

Two Jews were sentenced to death by the Nazis. A Colonel came up to them as they were about to be executed by a firing squad and asked, "Would you like a final cigarette?"

Jake replied, "You can keep your cigarette, you murdering no-good."

Whereupon his companion whispered to him, "Keep quiet, Jake. You want to make trouble?"

At a dinner party, the hostess served the appetizers herself, carrying the tray around to each guest. One man, however, declined.

"But you must!" insisted the lady.

"Really, they're delicious," replied the guest, "but I've had six already."

"Actually, you had seven," advised the hostess, "but who's counting?"

An anti-Semite challenged a Jew to a duel. At dawn the next morning the anti-Semite came to the appointed spot with his seconds. And they waited.

Half an hour later, the following message arrived from the Jew: "Unavoidably detained. Hate to disappoint you. So don't wait for me—go ahead and shoot."

# Polish Jokes

**A** woman was showing a contractor through the second floor of her new house, advising him what colors to paint the rooms. "I'd like the bedroom done in blue," she instructed.

The contractor walked over to the window and shouted: "Green side up! Green side up!"

"I want the bathroom in white." continued the woman.

Again the contractor yelled out the window, "Green side up! Green side up!"

"The halls should be done in gray."

Again the contractor shouted out the window, "Green side up! Green side up!"

"Everytime I give you a color, you shout 'Green side up!" the woman snapped angrily.

"I'm sorry, ma'am." the contractor explained. "But I've got three dumb Poles down down there below putting in the lawn."

**A** comedian asked, during his usual routine, "What's black and white and floats down the river on it's back?"

"The next comedian who tells a Polish joke," shouted a member of the audience.

Jane Paderewski had an uncontrollable longing to talk to her mother in Warsaw. She went over to the phone company, and told the girl at the front desk, she didn't have the money to make the call, and wanted to see the company's manager.

The manager ushered her into his office and Jane pleaded. "Mr. Jones, I just must speak to my mother. If you let me, I'll do anything, anything."

"Anything?" asked Mr. Jones.

"Yes, anything, anything!" insisted Jane.

"OK, Miss Paderewski," said Jones. "Come over here and kneel down."

Jane did as she was told.

"Now unzip my fly," continued Jones.

Jane did as she was told.

"Now take it out!"

Jane did as she was told.

"Ok, now you can begin," continued the manager.

Miss Padereswki grabbed on an called out "Hello, ma!"

How many Poles does it take to pull off a kidnapping?

Six.

One to kidnap the victim and five to write the ransom note.

A man walked into a butcher shop to buy a pound of brains. There were three piles. $1 a pound, $10 a pound, and $10,000 a pound.

"Why is the first pile only a dollar?" inquired the customer.

"Those are French brains!" answered the proprietor.

"How come the second bunch is $10?"

"Those are Negro brains," said the owner.

"Why is the other pile $10,000?"

"They're Polish brains!" explained the boss.

"But why are they so expensive?"

"Do you know how many Poles it takes to get a pound of brains!"

What's the first thing a Pole does when he gets out of the shower?

Takes off his clothes.

Harry, I got a great new Polish joke for you," said a cameraman to the floor manager.

"Okay, but just be careful," warned Harry. "Remember, I'm Polish!"

"All right," replied the cameraman, "I'll tell it to you very slowly."

## Color Blind

A Pole, a Black, and a Mexican, who were living together, were out of work. The Pole came home one day and said he had gotten a job. "Hey, fellows, wake me up tomorrow morning at five," he said. "I have to be at work by 5:30."

Then the Black said to the Mexican, "He got a job because he's white. We can't get a job because we're brown and black."

So during the night they put shoe black all over the Pole.

Next morning, when the Polish boy arrived at work, the foreman said, "Who are you?"

"You hired me yesterday," the Polack replied. "You told me to be here at 5:30."

"I hired a white man—you're black."

"I'm not!"

"Yes, you are! Go look in the mirror!"

The Pole rushed over to a mirror to look at himself, "My God! They woke up the wrong man!"

If there are thirty motorcycles going down the street, how can you tell which one the Pole is on?

The one with the training wheels.

**S**omski got an out-of-town construction job and asked his pal, Tom to check up on his wife to see that she didn't fool around with anybody.

Six months later he returned and found his spouse and his buddy in bed doing the very thing he had tried to avoid. Somski called his wife every name in the book and then threatened divorce.

"And as for you, you dirty dog," the Pole shouted at his best friend, "can't you at least stop while I'm talking to you!"

**W**hat do you get when you cross a Pole and a flower?

A blooming idiot.

## Not So Bad

"How far is it to Minneapolis?" Sigismund asked a station attendant.

"Twenty miles," he answered.

"In that case, we had better get going," said Alexis to his friend. "Twenty miles is a lot of walking."

"Not too much," answered Sigismund, "only ten miles apiece."

**A** lawyer in Rialto, California, swears that this story about Stanislaw Putsidwakim going to court to have his name changed is true.

"I can understand how you feel," sympathized the judge. "A name like Stanislaw Putsidwakim could certainly be a handicap. What would you like to change it to?"

"*George* Putsidwakim," said the Polack.

**H**ow do you make a million dollars in Poland?

Start with two million.

**W**ho was Alexander Graham Polowski?

The first telephone Pole.

**W**hat is the easiest job in Poland?

Intelligence officer in the Polish army.

**Z**big couldn't sleep at night, and in desperation he went to a doctor. The doctor told him if he couldn't sleep, he should count sheep.

The next day his friend asked him, "Say, Zbig, did you sleep last night?"

"No, I couldn't fall asleep. My adding machine made too much noise."

## Not Always

A matchmaker was exulting over the virtues of a particular girl. "She is beautiful, tall, well-built, a good cook, a smart woman, with integrity," she listed.

But the client said, "But you left out one important thing, didn't you?"

"Not possible!" said the matchmaker. "What could I have left out?"

"That she limps!" said the young man.

"Oh!" came the answer, "But only when she walks!"

An American regiment arrived in Africa. Sigismund Polski jumped off a camel, and took off his clothes right down to his shorts.

"Hey!" yelled the Sergeant, "what the hell do you think you're doing?"

"I'm going bathing," said Sigismund.

"Bathing!" screamed the Sergeant, "This is the Sahara. There's no water around here for thousands of miles."

"No?" answered Sigismund, somewhat perplexed, "With such a wonderful beach like this!"

How can you tell a Pole from a monkey? The monkey peels the banana before eating it.

Sigismund had just started his new job as a bus driver and he approached his work conscientiously. For five straight days, his fares totaled a steady $75. No matter how diligent he was, he always ended the day with the same $75.

The following Monday, however, Sig proudly handed the company cashier a pouch containing $314. The bus official was astonished. "Fantastic!" he said. "How did you do it?"

"It was easy," explained the Polack. "After five days on that terrible route, I figured business would *never* improve. So I drove over to 14th Street, and worked there. I tell you, that street is a gold mine!"

Stanley Saporski walked into an automobile showroom and asked the clerk how much a Cadillac would cost him.

"$9,000," answered the clerk.

Whereupon Stanley took out his wallet and handed the clerk nine $1,000 bills.

The clerk asked Stanley for his address and for other data, and then wound up saying, "Will we deliver it to you, or will you drive it out?"

"No," answered Stanley, "just leave it where it is. I'll never find such a good parking place anywhere."

**A** Pole was walking along a country road when he met a stranger.

"What have you got in that sack?" asked the stranger.

"Chickens," said the Pole. "And I'll bet you can't guess how many I got in here."

"Well, if I guess how many you got in the sack, will you give me one?"

"Sure," answered Stan. "If you can guess how many are in the bag, I'll give you both."

**A** man was carrying a great wardrobe down the street. A lady came up to him and said, "That's a terrible load. Isn't there anyone to help you?"

"Oh, yes," answered Stan. "My helper is inside the wardrobe carrying the clothes."

## What?

Sigmund was having a beer with his friend, Frank.

"My neighbor must think I'm in the Coast Guard," said Sig.

"Why is that?" asked Frank.

"Well, he keeps calling up my wife to ask if the coast is clear."

Stan's sister had just given birth. Stan was as proud as a peacock. He rushed over to the hospital, and, eager to determine whether the child was a boy or a girl, he asked the nurse, "Tell me, am I an uncle or an aunt?"

What do they call a Pole who sits in a tree?

A branch manager.

The ventriloquist sat on the stage and said, "I'm going to tell a Polish joke."

A Pole in the audience stood up and said, "No jokes about the Poles. We're not as thick as you think."

"Keep your shirt on!" said the ventriloquist, "What I say is nothing personal."

"I know that," said Sigismund, "I'm not talking to you either. I'm talking to that little fellow on your knee."

It was 4:00 a.m., and the phone rang. A voice said "Sig, this is John. Sorry to wake you up at this hour."

Sig replied, "Oh, that's all right, I was getting up to answer the telephone anyway."

# Russian Jokes

**A** much-decorated Russian hero returned from duty on the Finnish front where he had performed valorous service. He had been up in the mountains for months on end in the dead of winter. This was his first furlough in a full year.

A reporter came to see him. With a twinkle in his eye, the reporter asked, "Tell me, Captain Ivan Petrovich, what was the *second* thing you did after being away from your wife for a full year?"

Ivan answered without hesitation, "The *second* thing? Why, the second thing I did was take off my skis."

## This Is Not the Worst

Two neighborhood cronies were gossiping one morning when a third lady eagerly joined the group.

"Have I got a story!" interrupted the newcomer. "Poor old Linsky just tripped at the top of the stairs, fell down to the bottom, hit his head, and died."

"Died?" exclaimed the other ladies.

"Yes," asserted the talebearer. "And he broke his glasses, too."

Brezhnev paid his mother a visit. Wishing to impress her, he took her for a drive in his fine Zil limousine. She made no comment. Then he drove her to his spacious apartment, which was all carpeted with fine rugs and fitted out with the most modern equipment. Still she had nothing to say.

So he decided to drive her to his dacha. He showed off his private motor boat, hid dock landing, his swans, servants and all the other accoutrements of glory. She remained silent. Finally he said to her, "Well, what do you think of your son?"

"It's all fine," she said, "really fine. But I am worried. What will happen if the Communists come back?"

Ivan Petrovski was assigned as Russian Consul to some far-off island country. This involved a sea voyage which he loathed. In fact, he took the ocean crossing very badly and was suffering no end.

During the bitterest period, he was out on the deck leaning over the rail and retching miserably when a sympathetic steward tapped him on the shoulder and said, "Honorable Comrade, I know you're having a bad time, but just remember that no man ever died of seasickness."

Ivan Petrovski lifted his drawn countenance, now almost green, and addressed the steward as follows: "For heaven's sake, Comrade, don't say that. That is the last thing I want to hear. As a matter of fact, it's the wonderful hope of dying that's keeping me alive."

Harriet Gold loved borscht. One day, she was spooning herself a bowl of borscht when her pal, Abie, came to call.

"Harriet, I'm sorry to be the bearer of bad news," said Abie, "but Harry just got hit by a truck." Harriet kept on spooning her borscht.

"I don't think you heard me, Harriet," repeated Abie more urgently. "Harry's just been killed!"

Harriet kept on drinking the borscht. "I heard, Abie! I heard! As soon as I'm finished drinking this borscht, will I let out a scream!"

An 82-year-old woman tottered into Dr. Meyrowitz's office. "Doctor," she told her physician, "I'm not feeling too good."

"I'm sorry, Mrs. Kupnick, some things not even modern medicine can cure. I can't make you any younger, you know."

Mrs. Kupnick replied, "Doctor, who asked you to make me younger? All I want is for you to make me older."

In a little town in Russia, there were many more girls than boys. Consequently, the local matchmaker was having an easy time making good matches for the young men of the village, although the girls were often ending up with the poor end of the bargain.

A rather unpleasant man in the village, whose face matched his disposition, wanted a bride who possessed beauty, charm, and talent.

"I have just the girl for you," said the matchmaker. "Her father is rich, and she is beautiful, well-educated, charming. There is only one problem."

"And what is that?" asked the young man, suspiciously.

"She has an affliction. Once a year, this beautiful girl goes crazy. Not permanently, you understand. It's just for one day, and she does not cause any trouble. Then afterwards, she's as charming as ever for another year."

The young suitor considered. "That's not so bad," he decided. "If she's as rich and beautiful as you say, let's go to see her."

"Oh, not now," cautioned the matchmaker. "You'll have to wait to ask her to marry you."

"Wait for what?" pursued the greedy man.

"Wait for the day she goes crazy!" came back the answer.

"My wife," said Koblinsky, "is so educated, so well read, that she can talk for hours and hours on any subject you name."

"Huh," scoffed Yankelovitchnik "that's nothing. My wife can talk for hours and hours and doesn't even require a subject."

When he was before the committee of admissions, an applicant to a swank country club was asked, "Did your parents come from Russia?"

"No, they didn't," he answered.

He was elected to membership.

Two weeks later, he was brought back before the same committee on charges: "You lied when you were interviewed. We asked you if your parents came from Russia, and you said they didn't."

"No," said the applicant, "they didn't. They're still there."

A factory girl came up to her boss and said, "Madame Kruschenski, I would like to get off early this evening so I can attend the opera."

The boss lady got very angry. "Don't call me *Madame*," she said. "We have no bourgeois titles in Russia; we're all the same. Never use the word *Madame* to me again."

Then she called after her, "What opera are you going to see?"

"Comrade Butterfly," replied the girl.

It was the final night of the great Soviet Ballet performance in Leningrad. The house was packed. Some had come from far-off cities to view the season finale of Moscow's prima ballerina Yevna Ostrakhovna. The hall was agog with excitement.

Just before the performance, impresario Ivan Dostrovich came into the ballerina's dressing room, told her that the house had standing room only, and that this was to be the prime moment of her brilliant career.

The star, utterly exhilarated, performed magnificently, and rewarded her devotees with five different encores.

On the first encore, Yevna strode up the staircase to the first balcony, and while the violins strummed, she wafted herself from the rail directly onto the stage, and performed in a *pas de deux.*

For her second encore, she ascended to the second balcony, and as the drums beat a fanfare, she jumped into space and onto the stage, where she executed a perfect *arabesque.* The crowd went wild!

For her third encore, she climbed a rope to the third balcony, using only her hands. As the drums sounded a resonant roll, she leaped onto the stage, and performed in a *pas de trois!*

For her fourth encore, she was hauled in a silver basket up to the fourth balcony, whence she leaped through space onto the stage and executed an *entrechat!* The applause was deafening.

For her fifth and final encore, as the crowd held its breath, she mounted a motor scooter which ran on a single rail. The dazzling figure was sped up to the fifth balcony! Waving her hands to the enthralled audience below, she leaped into space, and landed on the stage in a *perfect split!*

Yevna didn't move. The crowd couldn't catch its breath! The feat, performed with such incredible grace, staggered the imagination! The audience hardly had enough energy to applaud.

But after a half-minute's utter silence, the hall broke into a thunderous roar.

At last, the curtain was drawn closed in finality. The audience departed. But Yevna remained on the stage, motionless. Her tear-stained manager appeared. Through it all, he had been rocked with emotion.

"Ivan!" cried Yevna, "Do me just one favor."

"Anything, Yevna! Anything! Tell me what you want, I'll do anything!"

Then, noticing that the ballerina remained motionless, he asked: "Yevna, are you hurt?"

"No, Ivan," she answered. "But I can't move. Just rock me a little, please, *and break the suction.*"

An impecunious cobbler lived in a tiny village near the Siberian border. His only concern was an incredibly ugly daughter whom he couldn't manage to marry off.

One day, a local matchmaker dropped in on him and let fall this bombshell: "I have a man for your daughter."

"Oh," exclaimed the cobbler. "Who is he?"

"Count Petrof!"

The cobbler was stunned. Count Petrof was the richest, the most handsome, the most aristocratic catch in all Russia.

The cobbler said, "No, no, I can't permit it. My daughter would be marrying outside her class, and I wouldn't want to be responsible for leading her into unhappiness. No, no, not at all!"

The matchmaker pleaded, but got nowhere. The old man would hear nothing of it. In desperation, the matchmaker said, "Well, we'll leave the decision up to the priest.'

The cobbler consented. After thinking it over for ten minutes, the priest said, "The match is all right."

The matchmaker was delighted. He snatched his briefcase and ran from the room.

The cobbler dashed after him, "What are you doing? Where are you going now?"

"Well," cried the matchmaker, "half my work is done. All I have to do now is convince Count Petrof."

# Scotch Jokes

**A** Scotsman signed up for a stint on a ship. In the middle of the voyage, the Scotsman and an Englishman were cited for committing an infraction of the rules. Each was sentenced to six strokes with the lash.

The captain said he regretted the sentence, but that rules were rules. Nevertheless, being a merciful man, he would permit each of the culprits to have something put on their backs before the punishment was inflicted.

The Englishman said he would like to have a piece of heavy canvas put on his back. His request was granted.

"Now, you," said the captain addressing the Scot.

"Well, me, as far as I'm concerned," said the Scotsman, "I would like you to put the Englishman on my back."

## Important Invention

How did the man who invented slow motion pictures get his idea?

One day, he watched a Scotsman reaching for a restaurant check.

A Scotsman was at a party. The host had his daughter sing some ballads. Beaming proudly, the father asked Jock Williamson, one of the guests, what he thought of the recital. "Doesn't she sing well?" asked the father.

Williamson was cornered, and could only nod assent.

The father continued, "And what do you think of her execution?"

"Well, man," answered Williamson, "I'm in favor of it."

McTavish, who was seated in a restaurant, waited an unconscionably long time to be served. When a waitress finally appeared with his order, McTavish greeted her with "Well, Lassie, it is strange but you don't even look a day older."

McFarland took his son to the theater. They were put in the first row balcony. The boy was so excited he leaned way over the rail.

"Careful now," said the father "don't lean too far over. You might fall and land in the pit, and it costs half a crown more down there."

McBride, on a visit to London, decided to go to the theater. He was intrigued by the title *The Forty Thieves.* But when he got to the box office he was taken aback by the price of the tickets, for two pounds was the charge for the cheapest seat.

The clerk at the wicket roused McBride out of his silence, and said "How many will you have?"

"Ah," answered McBride, "you can keep your tickets at two pounds each for *The Forty Thieves.* Now that I've seen you, I don't have to see the other thirty-nine."

McGovern, Professor of History, wrote the following note on his blackboard: "PROFESSOR McGOVERN WILL MEET HIS CLASSES NEXT TUESDAY AT 9:00 A.M."

One of the students, wanting to spoof the professor, crossed out the "c", so that the sign read: "PROFESSOR McGOVERN WILL MEET HIS LASSES NEXT TUESDAY AT 9:00 A.M."

Nothing daunted, the professor read the announcement, and crossed out the "l". The announcement now read: "PROFESSOR McGOVERN WILL MEET HIS ASSES NEXT TUESDAY AT 9:00 A.M."

## Big-hearted

MacDougal, a bear of a man, fell heir to a great fortune. His friends in the saloon were concerned that his sudden wealth would change him, would make him stingy. The boys were discussing the matter, when in dashed MacDougal. He waved them all to the bar. "When MacDougal drinks—everybody drinks!" he shouted.

After all had imbibed, MacDougal slapped a dollar on the bar, and announced: "And when MacDougal pays—everybody pays!"

## Possible Tragedy

An elderly Scotsman who was carrying a bottle of whiskey on his hip, slipped and fell on a wee patch of ice on the pavement. As he got up he felt something wet trickling down his leg.

"I hope it's blood," he murmured.

## Winning Words

A little boy asked his father to explain the difference between capital and labor.

"Well, son," the father replied, "if you lend money, that's capital. If you try to get it back, that's labor."

Two Scotsmen were playing golf. At the fourth hole, Sandy complained, "Mac, I do not feel well. Let's go back to the clubhouse."

Mac tried to brace up his friend, and told Sandy the air would do him good. But at the fifth hole, Sandy complained again, and said, "Mac, my stomach has gone wrong."

Mac once again tried to cheer him up and said, "Just take a deep breath and you'll be all right."

"But I do not feel right, I'm telling you. The fact is that at the fourth hole, I let out a fart."

"Ah," said Mac, "that can happen to any of us. Don't be alarmed."

"Ah," wailed Sandy, "but the trouble is—I followed through."

## Honi Soit Qui Mal Y Pense

Two business partners had never had an argument in 20 years. One week one of the pair came down with a virus and missed a few days at the store.

On the fourth day of his absence the ailing partner received a call from his associate, who told him, "I just found $1,500 missing from the safe. What should I do?"

His partner replied quickly, "Put it back!"

One devout Protestant had parked his car near the railroad station and was running as fast as he could to make a five o'clock train. Suddenly he saw his minister strolling along.

Out of breath from running, the traveler said a good-day to his pastor, and apologized for speeding by as he had to make the five o'clock train.

"Why, so do I," remarked the minister. "But we've plenty of time, plenty of time." he pointed to his watch. "See? We have twenty minutes."

The runner sighed in relief and walked more slowly alongside his minister. But when the pair arrived at the station, they found that their train had already left.

The minister was apologetic. "I had the greatest faith in that watch," he explained.

"I know," said the parishioner, "but what use is faith without good works?"

A Scotsman and his wife went on holiday, and during their travels in the countryside they ran across a small airfield which carried a sign, "Two pounds for a ride in one of our planes."

The aviator looked over the pair and decided they were Scottish. He realized he couldn't possibly get two pounds out of them. So he tried a ploy.

"Mister," he said to the Scotsman, "I will take you and your wife up for nothing on one condition. If you let out one word—no matter what—you pay me two pounds for the trip. If you're absolutely quiet, without a squeak, you ride free."

The Scotsman and his wife jumped at the proposition. They got in the plane, and the aviator went aloft. Then he began his tricks. He looped the loop, he rode upside down, he dived, he did everything he could think of. But there wasn't a sound from either of his passengers. As they landed, the aviator said, "You win, there wasn't a word from either one of you."

"No," said the Scotsman, "I didn't say a thing, but I came damned near talking when my wife fell out."

"There's nothing wrong with you," said the psychiatrist to his patient. "Why you're just as sane as I am!"

"But, doctor!" cried the patient, as he brushed wildly at himself, "it's these butterflies. They're all over me!"

"For heaven's sake!" cried the doctor, "don't brush them off on me!"

## Just Let Me Get My Hands on Him

It was on an outing from Edinburgh on one of those beautiful Scottish lakes. In the afternoon, the waters turned choppy. Suddenly, the launch keeled to one side and a beautiful young girl fell overboard.

For a few desperate moments, it seemed she was lost. Then, all of a sudden, a middle-aged Scot plopped into the lake and dragged the girl to safety.

The father of the beautiful miss embraced the weary Scot, and rung his hands in gratitude.

"You, Sir, you are a hero! You saved her life. How can I repay you?

"Just tell me one thing," said the dripping Scotsman, "Who pushed me?"

The old man was about to depart this earth. His sons had gathered at his bedside to discuss his funeral.

Jim said, "I can get twenty carriages to go to the cemetery for twenty pounds."

Timothy broke in, and said "We don't need that many carriages. I can get ten carriages, and they'll only cost ten pounds."

Walter then gave his opinion: "After all, a funeral is only a symbol, and I can get five carriages and they'll only cost six pounds."

At that point, the old man opened his

eyes and moaned, "If one of you lads will fetch my pants, I'll get up and walk to the cemetery."

A Scot, an Italian, and a Jew were dining together in an expensive restaurant. When the bill arrived, the Scotsman promptly declared that he would take it.

The next day the newspaper carried a headline: "Jewish Ventriloquist Shot in Restaurant."

McTavish and Blamey were having an argument. The Scotsman claimed that the Scots were lighter on their feet than the Irish.

"Ah, yes," agreed Blamey, "they sure are. And do you know how they got that way—it's because they learned how to tip toe out of the church when the collection plate was being passed."

Sandy had been in a train wreck. He collected 25,000 pounds, and his wife was awarded 10,000 pounds, too. His friends asked how it all transpired.

"Well," said Sandy, "despite the excitement, I retained my presence of mind, and I kicked her in the head."

Sullivan bounced into Clancy's saloon and he yelled out, "Clancy, give me three straight whiskies before the trouble starts."

Clancy poured the drinks and said, "Frank, what's the trouble, and when does it start?"

"Right now," answered Sullivan. "I haven't got a penny in my pocket."

Two friends walking down the street passed a church. Just then the bells started to peal. Mac said, "Angus, aren't they wonderful. They're so beautiful, the sound of those bells is so beautiful."

Angus turned to him and asked "What did you say?"

So Mac repeated, "The sound of those bells—aren't they beautiful?"

Whereupon Angus answered, "I can't hear a word you're saying on account of those awful bells."

# Swedish Jokes

**A** wealthy man decided to eat his lunch in the park one day to catch some rays of sun. Suddenly, an old man appeared, dressed in rags.

"Mister," entreated the poor man, "I haven't eaten anything for three days."

The rich man kept on eating.

"It's three days, mister, that I haven't eaten."

Still no response.

The beggar made still another try. "You hear—three days that no food has passed my lips."

The rich man was quite obviously annoyed as he put down his sandwich. "It's amazing. You yourself won't eat, yet you won't let me eat either."

## What Say You

Peter returned home early from a business trip and found his wife in the arms of his associate.

Reeling back, he exclaimed: "Max! I've *got* to. But *you*?"

"It's an outrage the way those nudists are carrying on in that apartment," the old woman told the policeman when he answered her call. "I'm ashamed."

The cop looked out the window and could see nothing but a vast courtyard, a road, and an apartment building in the distance. "I can't see a thing," he shrugged.

"Of course you can't," the old woman replied. "But just have a look through these binoculars and you'll see plenty."

The social worker was aghast. Here was a woman with ten children. She lived in a walkup apartment on the fourth floor. The place was squalid, and the kids were climbing up all over her. She seemed utterly exhausted. The social worker suggested that she get a play pen.

"What's a playpen?" asked the mother.

"I have an old one down at the office, and I will bring it to you as a gift."

A month later, the social worker called on this case again. "How do you like the playpen?" she asked.

"Oh," said the mother, "it's wonderful, just wonderful! Every afternoon right after lunch I climb into it, lean up against the fence and read a book, and the kids can't bother me."

America is the home of people of many ancestries. Most individuals are fiercely proud of their heritage.

At a Swedish-American Day parade in New York City, one citizen of Scandinavian descent was waving his banner wildly. A reporter asked him why he celebrated this event, when he was born right here in America.

"Every man loves his native land," observed the parader, "whether he was born there or not."

## Nuptial Athlete

They were on their honeymoon. The bride was so nervous in the bedroom that the glass of water in her hand trembled. It was very unfortunate, for the groom slipped on the floor, and pole-vaulted out the window.

## He Was A Smart One

All the businessman's relatives gathered eagerly for the reading of his will.

"Being of sound mind," his lawyer began to read, "I spent every last cent before I died."

A suburban lady entered an exclusive boutique to look for a hat. She tried on many, but none seemed to satisfy her. One was too large, one too wide, another too dressy.

Finally, the exasperated saleslady said sweetly to her, "I wish I had a dozen like you," and walked to the back of the store.

Another saleslady, who had overheard the remark, was puzzled. "Why on earth did you say that to that obnoxious customer?"

"Because," said the worn-out woman through gritted teeth, "I have a hundred like her, but I wish I had only a dozen!"

Mr. Swenson was explaining relativity. "It's very simple. If a beautiful blonde sits on your lap for an hour, it feels like only a minute. But if you sit on a hot stove for a minute, it feels like an hour."

Mr. Haglund then ingenuously asked, "From such nonsense did Einstein make a living?"

Nils and Lars took a trip to Paris. They couldn't read the menu, so they took a chance and pointed to an item, and the waiter brought them herring. Lars turned to Nils and said, "Can you imagine, in Sweden we have herring by the ton, so we have to come to Paris just to get another hunk of herring?"

And to make matters more exasperating, the guy at the next table was eating a choice *Chateaubriand* steak. After he swallowed the last morsel, he licked his lips and called, "*Garçon, encore!*" In a few minutes, the waiter brought him another sumptuous steak.

So Lars looked at Nils, and Nils looked back at Lars, and they both called out together, "Waiter, *encore!*"

Whereupon the waiter brought them another dish full of herring.

## The Toughest Way

A man walked into a brothel and asked to see the madam.

"What can I do for you?" she said.

"Well," he answered, "I'd like a girl who can do it the hard way."

The madam thought for a moment, took mental stock of her protegées, and said, "Mister, we have girls here who will do just about anything. Now, tell me—I'm sure we can satisfy you—but tell me, what's the hard way?"

"Oh!" the client answered loftily. "On credit."

A
HART
BOOK

GALAHAD BOOKS